THE HIGH PLACES

PRAYERFULLY RISING THROUGH THE SEVEN DIMENSIONS OF LIFE

BY DAVID SANZO

Dedication

To my precious wife, Angela. You are truly a "love angel." Thank you for being my partner in life and daring to dream with me. I love you. Baby, <u>come soar with me</u>.

The High Places
by David Sanzo

ISBN 0-9647343-9-7
For Worldwide Distribution
Printed in the U.S.A.

Spirit of Life Ministries
4830 Morwanda Drive
Roanoke, VA 24017
540-986-1590
Email: SpiritofLife89@hotmail.com

TABLE OF CONTENTS

A TAKE ON IDOLS!

Foreword

Another great book has been written by David Sanzo, this time about the insightful seven dimensions of life. Step by step this book will take you to the high places of God's great kingdom, to the upper echelons of the spirit world.

In travelling, we must watch for the signs that tell us where we are and how to get to our destination. So it is with the kingdom of God. Many ask me, "Where am I in the Kingdom of God? I need guidance." This book will answer your questions and give directions to the high places of God.

This book will be a great blessing to pastors and saints everywhere, as it has been to me. "God bless you" is my prayer.

T. W. Barnes

INTRODUCTION

Have you ever experienced a true "high"? I am not talking about one that is induced by drugs. I am talking about a high that comes from life at its best. Have you experienced a moment of ecstasy for no other reason than simply the joy of living life? I am not speaking of a high that is reached by negative, destructive means. I am not referring to highs that are artificially created. I am referring to a high attained by positive means.

One example (though temporary) of this high is the runner's high. It is that euphoric state you can enter while running where you no longer feel tired. You feel as if you could go on forever. Some people attain this "high" in other temporary settings, such as the rush you may feel while skiing down a mountain, jumping from an airplane, or having achieved some other dream. What about living a life that in itself is a high?

Some attain this high more often than others do. Some experience a greater degree of life and elation than others do. Is this because of certain activities they engage in or is it because of their mindset? Could it be something from within?

It is true that some people possess a greater quality of life than others do. Some grow to the majestic heights of the redwoods while others spring up in all the wrong places like a weed. Some experience great joy, peace, and happiness as to be the envy of all. Others experience great sorrow, boredom, and misery, whose life is usually considered worthy of avoiding at all costs. Some exude life even in the middle of great sorrow while others cannot find that exhilaration in the best of times except through some drug, entertainment, or some other temporary experience. How is it that some live a great life while others never get out of a miserable pit?

Vince Lombardi is noted for having said, "The quality of a person's life is in direct proportion to their commitment to excellence, regardless of their chosen field of endeavor." Our commitment to excellence is based on our view of life. What we experience of life is greatly related to how we view life.

On a small scale, whether we view the glass as half full or half empty affects our response to the situation. On a larger scale, how we view life will determine our words and our actions. This will influence how others respond to us. This, in turn, has an effect on our further responses to them and to life in general. And the cycle goes on. But it all starts with how we view life. "As he thinketh in his heart so *is* he" (Proverbs 23:7).

The view we have of life will determine the goals and ambitions we have. It shapes our desires and, therefore, our motives. It determines how much we are willing to endure before we decide we have pursued enough. It forms the foundation that decides the price we are willing to pay to reach higher.

How do we view life? Is ours an exalted view of life? Or is it a muddied sight? Do we look from the vantage point of the eagle or through the eyes of a worm?

I once heard a prophet refer to what he called "the seven dimensions of life." I did not pay much attention to it because I thought it was another one of those things somebody came up with to satisfy some preconceived outline. Perhaps it was some convenient little scheme that sounded good but was superficial. So I did not worry about pursuing the idea. In fact, I completely forgot all about it.

About four months later I was in the presence of another prophet when he made reference to the same thing. This time I took a little notice of it. Still, since they had been closely connected in their past, I regarded it as something they invented that was perhaps useful but of little value.

Over the next two years, I heard a couple of other powerful men of God in the Spirit refer to the seven dimensions of life. At this point my curiosity was aroused. I made some notes about the subject and filed it away.

The next four years took an interesting turn with regards to this particular concept. The only times I ever heard it referred to was when I was with men who had experienced extraordinary encounters with God. I began to ask some questions and to hold some conversations regarding it.

I was eventually led to some materials that detailed this concept in print. I suppose it is something of a miracle that I came into contact with one particular book since (according to what I have learned) it has been out of print for longer than I have been alive.

After this, I began speaking to certain individuals about this concept. What generally would start out as a five minute conversation would turn into an hour long discussion about it. Always they would ask to meet with me again to learn more about it. Often, I would be encouraged to write something about it.

This book is, in part, an answer to those requests. This book was initially supposed to be a part of my previous book, <u>The Key to the Kingdom</u>. But the concepts in that book kept growing until it became its own. So this concept, in turn, became a book of its own.

In Part I we will take a look at the seven dimensions of life. In Part II we will look at taking certain steps to rise higher in life effectively.

PART I

CHAPTER ONE

PREVIEW TO THE SEVEN DIMENSIONS OF LIFE

"We wrestle not against flesh and blood, but against principalities, against powers, against the rulers of the darkness of this world, against spiritual wickedness in high *places*" (Ephesians 6:12).

When we look back to where God first created man, we find that man was perfect (complete). Man was given a perfect genetic sequence and was able to enjoy life in much greater degrees than at present. The doors of his mind and spirit were open and clear.

When man was expelled from the Garden of Eden, he was removed from the higher dimensions of life. God did this not in anger but rather because of His mercy. It was done to protect man from being eternally separated from God.

It seems that most of humanity (in Western society) think that we are at a point where it is almost as good as it can get as far as our quality of life goes. At least many believe that it is better than it has ever been. That is why they settle for things on such a low plane. They measure life purely from a materialistic point of view. They think they are occasionally enjoying life. But their sights are set too low. Others simply endure life. It would be more accurate to say that they endure existence. This is because they rise no higher than the third dimension.

Most of humanity will live somewhere in the third dimension. We see that we are much better off than the animals who live in the first two dimensions. But we fail to see that we can rise so much higher.

Often, we tend to live in different dimensions in the various parts of our lives. However, there is still one dimension that

The creation of man

3rd dimensions

predominates our lives. That dimension, for most people, is the third.

As you read the following chapters, consider where it is that you spend most of your life. How do you view life? With a second dimensional mindset? With a fourth dimensional mindset?

Which dimension do you live in -- honestly? What types of powers and joys are manifested in your life? You may be doing well but would you like to do better? Why not rise up in God to be what He has designed you to be. Lift yourself to a higher dimension. It is not that we can lift ourselves entirely on our own but we can do it with God's help. Let God lift you up where you belong.

Preparing the Soil

As a child my hero was George Washington, the father of our country who showed great honesty in the cherry tree situation. I know what some of you are thinking. Why George Washington? Everyone else had heroes of every other kind. Most of my generation had heroes who were sports stars, movie stars, and rock stars. Their heroes were people who were alive. Mine had been dead for almost two hundred years. Somehow I chose George Washington for my hero. I looked up to him greatly.

I read every account of his life that I could. They were the first books that I devoured at any library I entered. In my childhood imagination, I fought alongside him in battle. My anger was kindled when he was angry. His sacrifices and his purpose in life inspired me. I wept when he parted with his generals at the close of the Revolutionary War.

I admired his overcoming personal heartache unselfishly in order to help establish a new nation which was much different than others existing at the time. I admired his purpose in life and the cause for which he fought. I was enamored by his ability to overcome the odds to achieve with purpose. To me, he could do no wrong. I would have gladly followed him into battle. This is the strength of moral authority in leaders.

It was particularly in the story of Valley Forge that I learned the greater the troubles, the greater the victory would be in the end. The harder the struggle meant the more wonderful the glory would be when you finally overcame.

I saw a measure of glorious living in the winter at Valley Forge. This was not because I wanted to endure hardship and suffering. It was because I wanted to be strong enough that nothing could deter me from reaching a greater goal, from possessing a grand purpose. I wanted to win great victories in life. And to win great victories you must fight great battles. Great problems must be overcome. Before you can triumph you must be in a situation where you have to try "umph."

I wanted the glory of triumph. The story of George Washington watered the seed for the pursuit of greatness in my life. It helped me to lift my sights to the higher levels of life.

Before we begin talking about the seven dimensions, I need to take a little more time to condition your mind to receive this understanding, to salt your oats and intensify your thirst for true life. Our minds must be prepared to receive high concepts just as the basics of elementary mathematics must be mastered before tackling higher mathematics.

Paul stated that "the natural man does not receive the things of the Spirit of God, for they are foolishness to him; nor can he *know* them, because they are spiritually discerned" (I Corinthians 2:14, NKJV). Jesus helped to prepare the minds of His listeners for His teaching by telling them to "Repent, for the kingdom of heaven is at hand" (Matthew 4:17). Repentance helps us to properly condition our minds for the working of the will of God in and through our lives.

Unconditioned Minds

If someone's mind is not properly conditioned to receive this concept, it becomes probable for them to finish reading this book and come to off base conclusions about what I have written which I have yet to imagine. It is possible for one person to explain a high concept and for another person to totally misinterpret what the first person was trying to communicate.

There is an old tale told from years ago about how the pope once decided that all Jews were to leave the city of Rome. Naturally, there was an uproar in the Jewish community about this edict. So the pope agreed that he would enter a religious debate with a single member of the Jewish race. If the pope won the debate, then the Jews would agree to leave. If the Jewish representative won the debate, then the Vatican would agree to let them stay.

Since they did not have a choice, the Jews began to look among themselves to find a champion to defend their faith.

However, no one was willing to enter the debate with the pope. The pope was a brilliant intellectual and highly educated. No one wanted to take the chance for being responsible for the expulsion of the Jews from Rome.

Finally they found an old man named Mosheis. He was not a man of great accomplishments. In fact, he was only a street cleaner. That had been his lifelong career. Since he was old and poor they figured he had the least to lose. They asked if he would be willing to debate the pope in this matter.

He agreed to engage in the debate with the pope. Only he stipulated one condition. Since Mosheis was not used to saying very much and was not in the least bit eloquent, he asked that neither side would be allowed to talk. He wanted it to be strictly in sign language or hand gestures.

Strangely enough, the pope agreed. The great day of the debate came and people flocked to the amphitheater to witness this event. Since they had agreed not to speak, the pope and Mosheis sat down facing one another with the crowd all around them.

They sat there looking at one another for a couple of minutes. Then the pope raised his right hand and showed three fingers. When Mosheis saw that, he responded by raising his right hand and showing one finger. The pope grimaced.

The pope then waived his fingers all around his head. Mosheis countered by pointing to the ground where he was sitting. The pope shook his head. As everyone watched, the pope proceeded to pull out some wine and a wafer for the communion. Mosheis answered by pulling out an apple. The pope then stood up and said, "I give up. The man is too good. The Jews can stay."

A couple of hours later the cardinals were in session and they questioned the pope about what had transpired at the debate. "I don't know," the pope replied. "I held up three fingers indicating the power of the trinity. He responded by holding up one finger to remind me there has always been only one God.

"Then I waved my hand around my head to signify that God was all around us. He then pointed to the ground to remind me that God was here present with us.

"Finally I pulled out the wine and the wafer to tell him that the communion could absolve us of our sins. He pulled out an apple to remind me that we are all guilty of original sin. He had an answer for everything I brought up so I just gave up."

About the same time the Jewish community was gathering around Mosheis to find out how he had managed to outmaneuver the pope. "Well," replied Mosheis. "He showed three fingers to tell me we only had three days to get out of here. I showed him one finger to tell him that there was not one of us who was leaving.

"Then," Mosheis continued, "he waved his hand everywhere to say that the whole city had to be cleared of Jews. I pointed to the ground telling him that we were going to stay right here."

"What happened next?" the Jews were eager to know.

"I don't know," replied Mosheis. "He just took out his lunch to eat so I took out mine. Then he got up and left."

It is possible for the same actions or the same words to send people thinking in two totally different directions. It all depends on their mindsets. I want your mind to be conditioned to receive this as much as possible so you will not be misled by wearing glasses that distort the picture I am trying to present. This is why I am taking my time presenting this concept to you. This is why we must be willing to take an honest look at ourselves and how we live our lives. Only then can God help us to rise higher.

Concepts as Tools

At times we make remarks about certain individuals who are particularly privileged to be able to "live the life." Perhaps we will refer to a particular life style and say, "Now that is truly living." If we saw someone really enjoying himself or herself we may respond with "That is living it up," especially if they are doing it in a way that we wish we could do it. People will do crazy things just to try to "really live." It is all in pursuit of a higher level of life.

There truly are varying levels of life. An insect is not to be thought of as living on the same level of life as a dog. A bug's life is not as fulfilling as a dog's life. And whatever we may say about living a dog's life, a dog does not have the same quality of life as a human being. Not even all human beings have the same quality of life.

The person who is trapped by their addiction to drugs or alcohol does not have the same quality of life as someone who can have a load of fun without having to resort to an expensive, destructive substance. The person living in poverty will not have the same quality of life as someone who is financially well off, all other things being equal. Even among those who are rich (all other things being equal), one who must work ninety hours per week does not enjoy his riches as well as someone who is able to spend time with family and friends.

Life can be divided into seven different levels. As a general education in America is divided into twelve levels or "grades" so life can be divided into seven levels. Actually, because each level is so vastly different than the levels above or beneath it, it would be better to say that life can be viewed in seven dimensions.

When I refer to the seven dimensions of life, I suppose I should make something clear. This is not a "law" which is supposed to be treated as doctrinal. I am not saying that life falls concretely into seven categories. This simply is a tool to be used in helping us understand the various levels of life.

We divide prophecy into various periods to help us understand it. We do the same with human history as well as with the various fields of science. Why cannot we do this with the spiritual world?

We do not have a firm grasp of the intricate workings of the spirit world. We are only able to "see through a glass darkly" (I Corinthians 13:12). Since we only know in part, we are only able to prophesy in part (I Corinthians 13:9). However, even though the concept is not doctrinal and has a theoretical base, it can still be of great profit to our understanding of the spiritual world.

We have divided the spiritual world into different "levels." Paul referred to the spiritual world in the plural on numerous occasions implying various "levels."[1] In dividing it into various levels, we want to make sure to use this idea as a tool in understanding, not a measuring stick of accomplishment and self-exaltation in comparison to others. We have no need for cultivating more pride.

In addition, this is not intended to be a comprehensive work on this concept. I am greatly indebted to the writings of Glenn Clark and others for introducing this concept to me. But I do believe the overview here in Part I will be insightful.

This concept could be viewed much like the four different temperaments we describe to apply to differing personalities. We refer to sanguines, cholerics, melancholies, and phlegmatics. Now these divisions of the human personality are not laws that box individuals into categories. They are simply tools we use to help us understand our strengths and weaknesses.

What we have done is cut a pie into four equal parts. With these temperaments, let's say that we have cut the pie with cuts that

---

[1] Ephesians 1:3, 20, 2:6, 3:10, 6:12, and II Corinthians 12:2).

crisscross "up/down" and "left/right" on the page. We could have divided the pie with cuts that crisscross diagonally on a page instead. It would not have been wrong to do so. In fact, we could have cut the pie in a "tic tac toe" manner if we had so decided. We could have divided our view of the human personality using different labels and divisions. It would not have been faulty, as long as we stayed in the pie of human personality to describe the human personality. We still have the full pie of the human personality.

Where we mark the divisions is not as important as recognizing the different parts and understanding them. In fact, there is no person who fits one hundred percent in any one category (no one is 100% choleric, 100% sanguine, 100% melancholy, or 100% phlegmatic). People come in combinations of these. The human personality is even fluid, so that it may undergo a measure of change over time or as the result of circumstances. But we still use the categories to help us in understanding the different sides to the human personality.

The same is true of viewing life through the seven different dimensions. Where we mark the divisions between one dimension and another is not as important as recognizing that there are some levels of living that are higher in quality than other levels of living.

So also these seven dimensions of life are fluid. The passage from one to the next is not necessarily instantaneous, though through the power and will of God it can be. It is often accomplished through the process of growth. A child does not suddenly become an adolescent on a particular day. It happens over time through a process of growth. So it is with going from one dimension to the next.

Better Life Begins at a Right Angle

The Bible tells us that we have an enemy who seeks to destroy us, that is the devil. "Your adversary the devil walks about like a roaring lion, seeking whom he may devour" (I Peter 5:8, NKJV).

Jesus told us that "the thief does not come except to steal, and to kill, and to destroy. I have come that they [THE SHEEP] may have life, and that they may have *it* more abundantly" (John 10:10, NKJV). Notice that Jesus is not interested simply in making sure that we have life. Rather, He desires that we may experience it more abundantly. He's talking about a greater quality of life, something that goes far beyond what man is able to find on his own. It is abundant life.

God has promised His people eternal life. This is not solely existing forever. The truth is that all people will exist forever. Some will live in heaven and some will live in hell. They will both last for eternity but the quality of life between the two will be vastly different, as opposite as night and day. It will be as different as light and darkness, as diametrical as life and death.

Jesus often spoke about an eternal life. This does not refer simply to an existence that never ends. It is referring to a quality of life that is ever on the upswing, ever getting better, far beyond what man can comprehend. It is a high quality of life.

In speaking of the seven dimensions of life, one understanding that we must always keep in mind is how each dimension is so much greater than the one below it. It is so much more alive, so vastly superior to the lower dimension. It contains much greater joys, love, and peace. It increases in quality not by mere addition but exponentially. It is so much greater because it is so very different. Its difference can be explained by saying that each dimension crosses the one beneath it in a perpendicular manner, as if to form a cross. We view each dimension as being at a right angle with the dimension beneath it.

Let us take the symbol for negativity, "-" (the subtraction symbol). If we will cross it in a perpendicular fashion, we will form a right angle. This changes the symbol of negativity into the symbol for positivity, "+" (the addition symbol).

Each dimension seems to directly oppose the one beneath it. However, in opposing it, it makes it so much greater. It is the same way that the higher law of aerodynamics seems to contradict the lower law of gravity. Yet, to fully possess the next dimension does not mean we have to abandon the "benefits" of the dimension we find ourselves in. Even though the bird is able to fly, it does not mean that he cannot land and walk the earth. We do not lose the lower dimension when we rise to a higher realm. It only appears this way because the higher realm overwhelms the lower dimension. And yet, this is a bit of a poor example.

The higher realm exercises its laws over the lower realm. It encompasses and permeates the lower realm. The higher law of aerodynamics exercises its power over the law of gravity. Gravity will pull everything downward. But if you utilize the law of aerodynamics, you can rise above the powers of gravity. The lower realm only limits the powers, benefits, blessings, and pleasures that are released more fully in the higher realm. The lower realms may have some of these things but they have them in a limited and inferior version. The higher dimensions have them in abundance.

We could look at different dimensions in relation to space. First, there is a point. Secondarily, there is a line. Third would be a plane. It is here that we find shapes of various sorts. It matters not whether it is a square or a circle, just so we have area and a closed perimeter. The next step would be volume so that we do not simply have length and width but we also have height or depth.

In each case, there is a tremendous change and growth that takes place. In each case, the difference is drastic. In each case, the old is overcome by the new. Yet, the old has not been lost entirely.

We could view man's habitations in this way as well. First would be a man's room (where he sleeps). Second is the totality of his home. Third would be the street he lives on. Next is the block he lives on. After that comes the neighborhood followed by the town, county, state, region of the country, nation, continent, hemisphere, and planet. Of course, you can take this much further out. But this will suffice.

Again, in each case, the old is but a minor part of the new. The old is inferior in comparison to the new. The street has his home plus several others. The neighborhood has his block plus several others. The state has his town plus numerous others. But truly this is growth that is severely hampered when compared with the seven dimensions of life. Space, after all, is of little significance in the spirit world.

Time can even be divided in a similar way with its seconds, minutes, hours, days, weeks, months, years, decades, centuries, etc. Yet time is but a handicapped shadow when compared to the seven dimensions of life. Time cannot compare to eternity.

The Higher Dimensions Liberate

The higher dimensions liberate us in power while the lower dimensions shackle us in captivity. The higher dimensions release a greater flow of love, joy, and peace. The lower dimensions limit their flow. In progressing from one sphere to the next, we do not forsake the "blessings" that may be seen in the lower sphere. In each case, you do not leave one revelation to follow another. Each new revelation is brought into balance with the old. Though the new is much greater than the old, it still does not abolish the old. When Jesus gave us the New Testament, He did not destroy the Old

Testament (or the Law of Moses). He came to fulfill the law (Matthew 5:17).

In each change, the new realm swallows up the old realm. We have a good example in the military. When someone gets promoted to General, they do not lose the authority they had in any prior rank. They still have the rank of sergeant, captain, lieutenant, etc. But the new rank swallows up and overwhelms the old rank.

In each case, the change is profound. The difference is tremendous. And the level of life is so much greater than the one beneath it. I want you to be mentally, emotionally, and spiritually conditioned to rise into the higher dimensions. As with any great concept, you must be prepared to receive the understanding.

You must recognize that perhaps you have not attained to the highest level possible. You must see that there is more to life than what you have seen. You must acknowledge that there is room for improvement in your life.

This acknowledgement cannot be general. It must be specific. I know of many people who can say that they are not perfect but yet cannot concede a single, specific point where they need to improve. The result is that they never get any closer to perfection than where they have been.

It can be easy for us to think that we have arrived at the top when all we have done is close our eyes to everything above us. The tree can deny that there are living things that move around by their own free will. They could convince other trees that they are only "seeing things." They could say, "These animals are there one moment but not the next. Therefore, they must be figments of our imaginations. Even if they did exist, they would not have the quality of life that we have because they have no roots."

But the truth is that the tree's refusal to believe does not change the fact that mobility is preferable to an inability to move yourself. There is a freedom that animals have that a tree does not have. There are pleasures and securities that animals can partake of that trees cannot.

So it is with those who would deny there is a dimension of life that is higher than where they live. The carnal man may deny the existence of a spiritual world because he does not know how to relate to it. But it is there nonetheless. And it influences him just as well.

Once you perceive not only the room for improvement but also the compelling need for it and the benefits that accompany it, then you can begin to work to excel in that specific area. Of course, this requires change. The most difficult part to swallow is that it requires that we ourselves must undergo the change as individuals.

You do not have to change if you do not want to. But if you do not change, then you cannot enjoy the benefits that accompany the change. What good is music if it cannot be heard? What good is light if it cannot be seen? And what good is a life if you cannot live?

Some are willing to change their jobs, their homes, and their careers in order to rise higher in life. Others change friends, churches, and mates. But most are not willing to change that which needs to change the most – that is, to change themselves.

Do not be afraid to change. Do not be afraid to rise higher than where you live. Have the courage to let yourself be changed into the image of Christ.

Do not be afraid to see where you really stand, where you really live life. Do not be anxious about laying aside your luxurious apparel to see yourself as God sees you. Lay aside the garments of pride, reputation, and image so that you can see the real you. You do not need the visions of grandeur. There is no need to scam yourself. Be willing to stand naked before God (Hebrews 4:13). Do not allow various talents and abilities to stop you from reaching God.

It has been stated that some change because they see the light while others change because they feel the heat. The Bible tells the story of how Zaccheus climbed up a sycamore tree because he wanted to see Jesus. Zaccheus was short and could not see Jesus without getting higher.

Other people that day wanted to see Jesus as well. Because they were taller, they did not have to climb up a tree to get a good look at him. Many undoubtedly were content to see Jesus afar off. But Jesus went home with the one who could not depend on his natural height.

The Bible also tells the story of the rich man who died and went to hell. He finally was willing to change his attitude about life because he felt the heat. Let us be among those who are willing to change because we see the light – the light of God's Word.

Let us not allow personal accomplishments and abilities to interfere with our getting a good look at Jesus. Let us do whatever is necessary to get closer to Him. Now that we have a foundation for understanding the seven dimensions of life, let us take a closer look at them.

CHAPTER TWO

THE LOWER DIMENSIONS

The world belongs to the one who is wise enough to change his thoughts, words, acts, life, and direction when brought face to face with the truth.

The First Dimension of Life

The first dimension of life is what we will call the dimension of the bug. We are bypassing the plant kingdom because even though they have life, they do not have a mind and cannot understand or make decisions. Theirs is simply a state of existence (just as a point in mathematics has no direction – it is simply "there"). They have no consciousness. Man is not able simply to exist because he has a mind. Therefore, our first level will consider the bug.

The normal place of living for a bug is found in one dimension. The mosquito lives only for food, procreation, and survival. These are his only true instincts in reference to quality of life. His world is controlled by sensation, by instinct. They are either attracted to stimuli or are repelled by them. Mosquitoes are not interested in anything else. They do not have hobbies or interests. They have no goals or love. Their world is controlled by stimuli. They follow the strongest stimulus present.

There are people who live in the first dimension of life. All they understand about life is food, sex, and a measure of survival. They are not interested in any other part of life. They want only to consume things into their bodies, release themselves sexually, and possess some vague resemblance of trying to survive.

These live only to the satisfying of the physical body. Among them you will find the individuals who have reduced their lives to alcoholism, drug addiction, and prostitution. These are not the only groups who have reduced their lives to living in the first dimension but they do give an adequate picture of the first dimensional mindset.

Just because someone chooses to live in some of these lifestyles does not necessarily mean they are lost in the first dimension. But if they do not overcome their problem they soon will be stuck in the dungeons of this low dimension. This is where they can no longer control their actions and their choices. They are driven to their destruction by their lusts. They cannot find a way out.

They may "always have sex on their minds." Or they may think about nothing except their next shot of whiskey or bit of crack cocaine. They may just exist through life as a "couch potato." They have no dreams, no goals, and no joys. They are snared into despair and despondency. They pursue no opportunities and experience no life.

Perhaps, they only live to eat. Surely it is not wrong to eat but to have your life reduced simply to eat is a miserable existence. To have to depend on a drug to make it through the day is a dismal existence. Yes, they live. But their level of life is the lowest.

The normal place of man is in three dimensions. But man often does fall back into being limited to the lower dimensions. The insane man lives in a single dimension. He is abnormally focused on a thing of low degree. His life is not complete as is understood by most of humanity. He is alive. But his quality of life is greatly diminished from its possibilities and design.

Controlled by Fleshly Desires

The mathematical equivalent of the first dimension is a line. Bugs have only one direction to go and that is forward. They do not stop to contemplate their direction or their decisions. If there is a mountain in their way they will simply find a way around it or over it. If they cannot find a way, they go to the next stimulus that takes over their thinking process. They will continue to move in the direction they are driven.

Place your foot down in the path of an ant as it travels to find and bring a morsel of food back for the colony. The ant is not deterred whatsoever. It will simply go around your foot and continue doing its assignment. This is not because it understands the value of determination. They do not know discouragement.

They simply go in the direction of a line. They follow their instincts. They are ruled by their desires.

Bugs go where they are driven. If they see a light or a fire and are attracted to it, they will follow their compulsion to it. They are almost powerless to escape it.

> *The modern axiom "If it feels good, do it" is an invitation to lock yourself into the prison of the first dimension.*

They will head towards it and lose their life.

It is common practice to hang an electric light outside at night during the summer. We do this to help us deal with the problem of bugs. Gnats see the light and are attracted to it. But their attraction to it will cause their destruction. Moths will fly into it and get zapped.

They cannot understand that there is danger waiting for them. They cannot concoct a plan to escape it. They are driven to their death by their desire to get close to the fire. They are ruled by their desires.

The first dimensional people are controlled by every desire that their flesh has. They do not stop to consider the morality of their impulses. They are almost unable to avert their own destruction. Often, they cannot even understand that they are caught in a downward spiral toward ruin.

Take the case of those who habitually view pornographic materials. If you stop them from obtaining these materials one way, they will find another way. Even if they do not succeed in getting them,

> *When we allow ourselves to wander into the rooms of the first dimension, Satan likes to come behind us and lock the door.*

They will turn every interaction with a person as an opportunity to find sexual gratification. So they look at women with lust ruling their minds. They make comments, which make the ladies around them feel uncomfortable. They are lewd in word and deed.

Their carnal desires control them. This is the role of the lusts of our flesh. The modern axiom "If it feels good, do it" is an invitation to lock yourself into the prison of the first dimension. When we allow ourselves to wander into the rooms of the first dimension, Satan likes to come behind us and lock the door.

Lord of the Fly

Interestingly, one of the names for the devil is Baalzebub. This name literally means, "lord of the fly." When we settle for living in the first dimension, we have allowed the devil to become lord of our lives.

> *Life in the first dimension is that of a slave with our lusts being the whip that the taskmaster (Satan) cracks.*

When Satan is lord, we have no choice but to move in a direction directly ending in our death and destruction. We are moving straight along the line. We are following our instincts or the desires of our flesh. We are ruled by this mindset. We are locked into bondage.

We cannot swerve to the left or to the right. We cannot change direction. The wages of sin is death. We are moving in a straight line, which ends in death. We are driven as the gnat to the light. This is the life of a slave with our lusts being the whip that the taskmaster (Satan) cracks.

Sometimes when a murder is committed, the murderer is later shocked to know that they could perform such an act. They may try to plead insanity, or perhaps temporary insanity. It may even work for them in a court of law. But the truth is they have allowed themselves to slip into the first dimension. They have been caught in this first dimension where Satan can have his way in their lives. At the time of the murder, their flesh demanded compensation for whatever reason. They caved in to the demands of their carnal nature.

Another example is the man who loves his wife but beats her. Afterward, he is sorry he did it and promises never to do it again. He does not want to do it again. But he will because he is living in this lowest dimension. When the compulsion (lust) is there to vent violence, he is driven to do it again.

Amazingly, the lifestyles that certain elements of Hollywood and this world system often promote as "really living" and "being the life" to live are the ones where you are caught in a downward spiral. Living in the fast lane often means living in a fast-moving, downward spiral. The "high life" often is actually a fast road leading to a very low (miserable) life. "Happy hour" usually only destroys hope for happiness.

The major climax or goal of so many movies, conversations, books, etc., is to hop in bed with some other character in the story or to otherwise obey everything your flesh tells you it wants to do. In a higher dimension, this is not the height of life. It is but one of many pleasures of life that God affords us as long as we keep it in its place (as defined by the Word of God).

This world's value system glorifies the easy, the comfortable, and the convenient. Being a couch potato is spoken of as having no worries or problems and, therefore, ideal. People glamorize times of "vegging out." They want to do nothing but exist. This is miserable living. I am not talking about taking times of rest which Scripture advocates as being good for body, soul, and spirit. I am talking about that which stems from slothfulness.

There is no joy in mere existence. The tree does not know joy. God is not interested in seeing us decay from within. He does not want us to be held captive. He wants us set free. "If the Son makes you free, you shall be free" (John 8:36). Jesus came to "preach deliverance to the captives" (Luke 4:18).

As far as relationships go, the first dimensional people are only concerned with themselves. Their space consists only of their individual person. They can only think of "me, myself, and I." Their only interest in others has to do with those who will help them to satisfy their flesh. They have no use for those who do not fulfill this role. They can neither love nor care for people because they understand no other value than the lusts that drive them.

So the drug addict is only interested in people that can help her get some more drugs. The alcoholic will befriend anyone who will get

> *Their only interest in others has to do with those who help them to satisfy their lustful desires.*

him another drink. Others will hang out with anyone who will give them sexual pleasure. As long as the other party is willing to go to bed with them they will be considered an "item." This is the thinking of the first dimension.

Sometimes these poor souls are drunk with the wine of laziness. Fear and paranoia may have paralyzed others. They are shut in to their own world. The walls they build for protection are actually used for their captivity.

They may not know any measure of enjoyment. Depression is their best friend. They live life in a comatose state, barely existing from day to day. The only life they know is what they watch on television. Their life is empty. They sing a monotonous melody. They are corpses who are not quite dead. This is the miserable living of the first dimension.

The time equivalent of the first dimension is the "right now", the present moment. They only live for today's high, for the feel-good feeling right now. They are not concerned with next week or next month. They are cut off from the past and the future of this mortal life. They only want to get immediately whatever it is they presently desire. They will sacrifice the future if they can satisfy their lust right now.

Esau allowed himself to fall into the first dimension when he sold his birthright to Jacob for a pot of lentil soup. The great blessings attached to the birthright did not matter to him. He only cared that he would have something to eat while his body demanded it. He sacrificed a great future benefit because he had allowed himself to fall into the first dimension. The power, prestige, and riches connected with the birthright were traded to escape a few hunger pangs.

> *They will sacrifice the future if it means that they can satisfy their lust right now.*

People still do the same thing today. When they fall into one-dimensional thinking, they will sacrifice a great career in sports for some temporary high. They will trade a great business career for a shady agreement which excites their greed. They will swap a great marriage for an hour of forbidden pleasure. They will live to regret it. But they snared themselves into the first dimension. While in this low-level mindset, they become slaves of the immediate because they cannot see the ultimate.

Human beings often start their life in this low level of living. As infants, we are only interested in getting our next meal and being able to sleep. Other people's comforts are of no concern to us. We want our meal when we are hungry -- even if someone else has to wake up at two in the morning and lose sleep over it.

Infants' lives are guided by reaction to stimuli. They cannot give to a conversation. They can only smile and laugh at others. A week from now is of no interest to them, much less a month from now. They only know what they desire for the present moment. They have no goals for the future. This is not to disparage them. They are only babies. We do not expect anything more from them as of yet.

If life were a parade, the first dimensional mind would look only at the flute, the trumpet, or any particular instrument. They would think that sound came from the flute alone, not understanding that there is someone blowing wind into the flute. All they notice is the stimulus.

The Second Dimension of Life

The second dimension is what we will refer to as the dimension of the dog. The normal place of living for a dog is in two dimensions. A dog has the interests of the first dimension -- survival, food, and sex. But a dog has another dimension to him. He wants to have you as his friend. He wants you to play with him, to spend time with him -- even if you are not satisfying his first dimensional desires. He can find happiness if you are playing a game of "Fetch" with him.

In viewing a parade, the second dimensional mind would see not only the flute but also the person playing the flute. They may notice the face blowing wind into the instrument and the fingers dancing on its body. They notice the human being behind the instrument. This is the social realm.

The second dimension encompasses the social scene. Some people are social butterflies. They always want to be in the middle of the crowd but they have no depth to them. They will work to go to every party or social function. I am not talking about personality traits here. I am talking about motives and consuming desires. I am talking about mindsets. What dominates their goals, time, and energy is socializing.

The time equivalent of the second dimension has expanded considerably. They view life with a perspective that is anywhere from a few weeks to several years (usually around five to seven years at the most). They are still very limited to the present and the short-term future. It is hard for them to envision the distant future. It seems so far away that they almost believe it will never come.

A young adult thinking in the second dimension would not have an eye toward the retirement years, much less begin to plan accordingly. They will limit their planning to some upcoming gathering or event. They cannot relate well to planning for ideas, concepts, etc. Perhaps they only see the next couple years or so with their career. At best they can only see graduating from high school or college. They do not envision much past this event. It all seems rather vague to them. Getting old seems so far away.

Their sphere of relationships is expanded considerably from the first dimension. Instead of being limited to themselves, their space now includes friends and/or family. Still, it is a relatively small group.

They are not nearly as selfish as the prior dimension just as a dog is more thoughtful and less selfish than a bug. This is why a dog can be trained to help individuals with various tasks. This is why a dog can act on his own to defend his master. His love and loyalty for his master motivate him to help his owner.

Those in the second dimension have their own circle of social friends about whom they are concerned. Their motto is "Us four and no more" because they can see no more. They can relate only to their little group. As a dog has no concept of life one hundred miles from his present location, so these individuals do not consider life beyond their immediate environment.

These workers are only concerned about their department. The only class that matters to these students is their class. The only people that matter are those in their age group, race, income bracket, etc. No one is right if it is not his or her group. Anyone who does not directly fit in his or her life is not deemed important.

Loyalty may be strong but it is extremely shortsighted. They only consider the temporary and their immediate circle. Anyone who is of any significance must be in their gang, on their ball team, or in their club. No one else matters or is of any significance. The only problems are those belonging to their little group. The only victories are those belonging to their little group. The only opportunities of any value are those open to their little group. The rest of the world is considered a vague, abstract theory. They only understand what they see, hear, and otherwise experience.

> *The only problems, victories, and opportunities some people recognize are those found in their little group.*

If they read, it will usually have to do with the social scene. The magazines they read will tend to be about people who live superficial lifestyles. They are consumed with interest about the latest events in the lives of actors, entertainers, sports figures, etc. Other articles are considered boring. This is also true for the majority of the books they read and the things they watch. They get caught on the train of soap operas. The point here does not refer to those who occasionally find an interest in some of these things. It refers to those whose time and thoughts are devoured with these things.

The First Right Angle

The mathematical equivalent of the second dimension is a plane. Keep in mind that each dimension is at a "right angle" to the one beneath it. They seem almost to oppose it. They "contradict" it directly. The first dimension is concerned with things. The second dimension is concerned with people. The higher realm intersects with the lower realm. Being concerned with people often "opposes" concern for things.

The first dimension's mathematical equivalent is a line. The second dimension has another line that crosses it at a right angle. This gives us a plane. Here we can form shapes. Now we have a perimeter and area. We are not forced to travel forward. We are free to turn aside to the left or the right.

If you have ever walked a dog without a leash, you have seen that they did not necessarily walk the straight path with you. They went to the left. They went to the right. They were in front of you and behind you. They circled all around you as they explored everything that caught their attention.

They can avert danger more easily because they can see so much better than in the lower realm of the bug. The dog can see the fire and understand that it is very hot. They know that it provides warmth against the cold. But they also comprehend how, if they get too close to it, it will burn them. So they understand that they must keep a safe distance. They can override a measure of their instincts, their desires.

They can make choices about what they prefer. They are not driven into the fire by an unstoppable force within. They can turn aside. They can choose whether to chase a squirrel or come get the bone that you are calling for him to receive. An animal can overcome their impulses to jump wildly at some prey and wait patiently until they are sure they can succeed at the hunt. A dog can overcome his impulse to eat the piece of meat placed on his muzzle until his owner gives the command because he so desperately wants his owner's approval and friendship.

However, the dog does not enjoy restraining some of his desires. He will struggle within himself to hold himself still with the meat on his nose until the owner says it is okay to indulge in it. It takes all of his power to control himself. He will often whimper while doing it. He does not enjoy the restraint. Still, this level of living is so much superior to the prior dimension of the bug. He is able to override certain impulses. He has a measure of control over his desires even though his sights remain low.

People in the second dimension do know right from wrong. They understand good and evil in a measure. They respect the law (both of God and of men). They may even obey it. But it goes against every desire in their body. Every fiber of their being revolts against it.

Often they will give in to the urge to obey their flesh. This is especially so when authority is not present or they believe that no one sees their action. Paul talked about this inward struggle in Romans 7. He talked about how he often did what he did not want to do. He needed help being delivered from "the body of this death." He found this help in Jesus Christ.

Children usually live in this second dimension. No longer are they interested only in eating and sleeping as they were in the infant stage. Now they want to play. They have discovered the joy in simply having some fun. They want to have friends with whom they can spend time.

One of their greatest threats to friends who displease them in some manner is "I won't be your friend no more." If they want their friend to do something that is pleasing to them they may promise "I'll be your best friend for the rest of your life."

They want to please Mommy and Daddy. You can now appeal to them to do what is right or to do what will make someone happy. They can be taught right from wrong. They can make choices. They have preferences. They have grown from the stage of the infant. They have found the second dimension.

The Third Dimension of Life

We may well refer to the third dimension as the dimension of man. The normal place of living for secular man is in three dimensions. The third dimension is the dimension of time and space. It can also be seen as the dimension of knowledge.

Human beings have the interests of the first two dimensions. They are interested in food, sex, and survival. They desire to have friends and a social life. But they have yet another side to them. They have an intellectual desire. This dimension encompasses the world of knowledge and understanding.

As humans, we are encouraged to "get an education." We have a thirst for knowledge. We want to know what makes things tick. We desire to learn. So we go to school. We read books and articles. We listen to tapes and watch videos. We research subjects. We perform experiments. We observe our environment with the intent to learn. We like to explore. We learn how things operate. Our thinking is dominated by the idea of *analysis*.

Our reading is not limited solely to the superficial events in people's lives. It now includes information. Reading is used to learn facts, skills, and opportunities.

The mathematical equivalent of this realm is a cube. This dimension crosses the prior dimension "at a right angle." So we take a new plane and intersect it with the old plane. Now we have volume. Not only can we now turn left and right, we can go up and down.

Human beings are the only creatures that explore areas that are not directly related to them. We like to learn about faraway places and lands. We like to travel clear across the state, the nation, and even the world to see people and things that have no direct relationship with us. We explore not only the landmass on which we live (our natural habitat) but we also explore the depths of the sea and the heights of the heavens. We learn about the fish and the stars. We go both up and down.

Man is able to reason and understand. Therefore, when he sees a fire, he does not fly directly into it like the moth does. He does respect it like the dog does. But he can do better than that. With his reason and understanding, he can actually build his own fire and use it for heat or for cooking. He can use fire to work all types of services, such as refining metals. This is a whole new world, a brand new dimension.

In viewing a parade, the third dimensional mind will notice not just the individual musician but also the whole row of musicians. In fact, his perception goes much further than this. He perceives the different instruments present in the band. He notices the various sections of the band (brass, woodwinds, percussion, etc.). He can see the different segments of the parade.

Here we see another element of this dimension. The third dimensional man can understand that each musician, each band, and each float all have their own purpose in the grand scheme of the parade. Each individual and each section of the parade was designed for a purpose.

Introduction of Purpose

Purpose begins to be found here in the third dimension. No longer is it sufficient to settle for food, sex, and survival alone. In fact, just having some friends to socialize with is still not enough. Now we come to understand that a life with purpose is so much more fulfilling.

So we begin to make goals of things we would like to achieve. These goals, however, are limited in degree because of other limitations of this realm. Such limitations include (but are not limited to) the time limitations.

The time equivalent of this dimension is greatly expanded from the prior world. Here we have expanded our horizons from a few short years at best to include our whole lifetime. So we begin to plan for our families. We start making long term career moves. We initiate our retirement plans.

Whereas beforehand our goals were short term in nature, now they include lifelong projects. So we set out to build a strong business that we can turn over to our children when we are gone. We build cities, roads, and factories. We establish schools and hospital systems. We form organizations to carry out purposes that will endure for years to come.

We now have a past and a future. We want to know our roots. We like to learn history. We want to see historical monuments. We also are intrigued about what the world will be like in the future. We are concerned about the future of our children.

Coupling the desire for knowledge of the past with our eye to the future, we may even be interested in constructing a monument to ourselves so that we may be remembered and recognized. We may decide that we want to be historically significant. We now want to be noted for accomplishing some purpose.

In the first dimension we are trapped to the desires of the flesh. In the second, we understand right from wrong. We are still ruled by the flesh for the most part but we have a say in overcoming certain temporary desires. In the third, we can make conscious decisions to break certain habits and to establish other habits and disciplines.

The space of relationships in the third dimension is greatly enhanced from its prior condition. In math we went from a plane to a cube. Here our space goes from a small circle of friends to a great network of friends and associates. Now we include not only our own business but also the whole industry. We consider not just the local town but the nation as a whole.

However, even though we see much more, now we begin to have strong distinctions. We have a loyalty to our nation versus the other nations of the world. We have a stronger loyalty to our state and an even stronger one for our city. We prefer that our own state gain the new manufacturing plant with 10,000 jobs rather than the state on the other coast. We work for our city to open the international airport rather than the neighboring city. We root for our town's ball team rather than some other.

We will have a stronger loyalty yet towards our own company and circle of friends. Usually, the strongest allegiance follows the family bloodlines or some close friend. But we have made distinctions between people.

Divisions are Accentuated

We now make distinctions between all types of things. Knowledge abounds so we need order of some kind to keep track of everything. We begin to organize everything we have learned into subjects. Everything becomes classified into various categories. Everything is placed into its own place. Divisions are drawn.

The cube is limited in its space. It is solid and stationary. It resists change. The cube is exclusive of whatever is on the outside of it. It is distinct from all else that is around it. It encompasses its own space. It contains its own "territory."

Borders, therefore, are created. Boundaries are established. Everyone now has their own territory. Nations have their own lands. A border of some kind limits every authority. We move to protect what we consider as belonging to us.

A possessiveness now moves in. "What is mine is mine and don't you touch it without my permission." This possessiveness is not as selfish as that of the lower dimensions. It is not based on immediate satisfaction. It is based on what is perceived as rights, laws, and ethics. We develop a system of laws, regulations, and ordinances.

We have personal property and real estate that belongs exclusively to us. If someone else takes our belongings without our permission, we feel violated. We call it robbery. That person is classified as a thief.

If someone has something we desire but cannot obtain (or are unwilling to work to achieve), then we begin to resent it. We wish we could have it. Worse, we may begin to find a way to get them to lose it. If only we could concoct a plan whereby the desired possession would be considered ours rather than theirs, we would do it. Perhaps we formulate a plan to swindle it from them. If that fails, we could always try extortion. This introduces a new level of sin. These are not just sins of the flesh but sins of the mind. The internationally acclaimed T.F.Tenney has stated that each new level brings new devils.

Paul said that "we all once conducted ourselves in the lusts of our flesh, fulfilling the desires of the flesh and of the mind, and were by nature children of wrath, just as the others" (Ephesians 2:3, NKJV). But we are not allowed to continue like this as a child of God.

"This I say, therefore, and testify in the Lord, that you should no longer walk as the rest of the Gentiles walk, in the futility of their mind,

"having their understanding darkened, being alienated from the life of God, because of the ignorance that is in them, because of the blindness of their heart;

"who, being past feeling, have given themselves over to lewdness, to work all uncleanness with greediness.

"But you have not so learned Christ" (Ephesians 4:17-20, NKJV).

Because their heart was not right with God, God gave them over to degenerate in the quality of their life to lower and lower dimensions. Paul clarifies this in Romans 1 (more on this in Chapter 11).

The Work of Sin

When we refer to "being saved from a life of sin" we are usually referring to being delivered from life in the first two dimensions. Sometimes we include the third dimension as well. In a theological sense we may be referring to our fleshly nature inherited from Adam's fallen state, which, of course, is what drives us to being snared into the lower dimensions. "Then when lust has conceived, it bringeth forth sin: and sin, when it is finished, bringeth forth death" (James 1:15).

In a "practical" sense we often are referring to being delivered from being trapped in the first two dimensions (sometimes the third is included). When we refer to "living in sin" we often mean the mindset of the first two dimensions (with all of its accompanying actions). But we must be careful lest we allow ourselves to think that the third dimension is acceptable with God.

Actually, sin is anything that holds us back from God and the life which God has designed for us. If we are growing from the second dimension to the third, then everything that stops us from going towards that third realm of life is sin to us for it keeps us from reaching the higher life. It does not mean that everything in the third dimension is okay. But God may tolerate it until you can surpass it to reach the abundant life that Jesus talked about. More on this in Part II.

The Apostle Peter explained how these lower worlds are not where we are designed to live. Even though the world may think it strange that we will not degenerate with them into the first two dimensions, we are to go beyond these lower life styles.

"For we *have spent* enough of our past lifetime in doing the will of the Gentiles -- when we walked in lewdness, lusts, drunkenness, revelries, drinking parties, and abominable idolatries.

"In regard to these, they think it strange that you do not run with *them* in the same flood of dissipation [THE KING JAMES VERSION CALLS IT 'THE SAME EXCESS OF RIOT'], speaking evil of *you*" (I Peter 4:3-4, NKJV).

They will speak evil of you for not drifting into the lower dimensions with them. They mock you and make fun of you. They will try to intimidate you from seeking the greater life. They cannot understand that you are not willing to place your hands into chains that shackle them. Paul showed us that we have been delivered from being trapped in these first three dimensions.

"Do you not know that the unrighteous will not inherit the kingdom of God? Do not be deceived. Neither fornicators, nor idolaters, nor adulterers, nor homosexuals, nor sodomites,

"Nor thieves, nor covetous, nor drunkards, nor revilers, nor extortioners will inherit the kingdom of God.

"And such were some of you. But you were washed, but you were sanctified, but you were justified in the name of the Lord Jesus and by the Spirit of our God" (I Corinthians 6:9-11, NKJV).

We have been changed from our past condition of living in the three lowest dimensions mentioned here. We have been born again. We have entered a new realm of living, far superior to what we had known before. We have seen the dawning of a new day. Our eyes have been opened. We are no longer the same.

We no longer live as slaves to one degree or another to our fleshly nature. We are not forced to perform the works of the flesh. Paul described the works of the flesh (the results of being led by the impulses of our carnal nature) as follows.

"...adultery, fornication, uncleanness, lewdness,
"idolatry, sorcery, hatred, contentions, jealousies, outbursts of wrath, selfish ambitions, dissensions, heresies,
"envy, murders, drunkenness, revelries, and the like; of which I tell you beforehand, just as I also told *you* in time past, that those who practice such things will not inherit the kingdom of God" (Galatians 5:19-21, NKJV).

Paul told the church that some things should not even be named among the saints. We are living on a higher plane. Why should we backtrack to these sinful conditions?

"But fornication and all uncleanness or covetousness, let it not even be named among you, as is fitting for saints;
"neither filthiness, nor foolish talking, nor coarse jesting, which are not fitting, but rather giving of thanks [PRAYER].
"For this you know, that no fornicator, unclean person, nor covetous man, who is an idolater, has any inheritance in the kingdom of Christ and of God" (Ephesians 5:3-5).

Lest we get the wrong idea that sin is limited to the first three dimensions, let me say that it is not. As we move up into each new dimension we find a greater power and quality of life. We get closer to where God dwells. Therefore we become purer. Eventually sin is eliminated.

Nevertheless, sin has not been confined to the first three dimensions. Sins of the flesh (and some of the sins of the mind) are understood in terms of the three lower dimensions. But we still must wrestle against spiritual wickedness in high places. We still must cleanse ourselves from the filthiness of the spirit (II Corinthians 7:1).

"Deliver us, Lord Jesus, from the captivity of the lower dimensions. Lift us up from the miry clay and set us free. Break every chain. Lead us out of our prisons. Undo the heavy burdens. Keep us from being enslaved by our sinful nature. In Jesus' name."

CHAPTER THREE

THE INTERMEDIATE DIMENSION
The Fourth Dimension of Life

The fourth dimension is the dimension of motion. It is not limited to time and space. Here we have a whole new world. This is a much greater dimension with much greater power. This dimension is where we find the beginning of the spirit world.

The mathematical equivalent of this dimension goes beyond spatial dimensions. This dimension has to cross the third dimension at a "right angle." It must work somewhat opposed to the dimension below it. So whereas the third dimension is as a cube and is therefore solid and stationary, the fourth is in motion. Whereas the cube of the third is resistant to change, the fourth dimension is ever moving, always fluid, and in constant change.

The cube is limited in space, but the fourth dimension is not limited by physical space. The cube is exclusive of whatever is on the outside of it. It is, therefore, resistant to change. A mathematical cube will remain a cube. Its space is determined. On the other hand, the fourth dimension is inclusive and is all about change.

Just as width is perpendicular to length and volume is perpendicular to area, so the new world is perpendicular to the old. It seems to counter the world beneath. The third dimension is very strongly about material things in a temporal world. It is very much about division and the concrete world. The opposite of a physical world is a spiritual world. The spiritual world runs counter to the physical world.

If we concentrate our attention on non-spiritual things, we will reap the rewards of the lower dimensions – death and destruction. If we focus our energies on spiritual things, we can gain real life.

> "For they that are after the flesh do mind the things of the flesh; but they that are after the Spirit the things of the Spirit.
>
> "For to be carnally minded [FOCUSED ON THE LOWER DIMENSIONS AS THE CENTER OF OUR BEING] *is* death; but to be spiritually minded *is* life and peace.
>
> "Because the carnal mind [THE LOWER NATURE AND MINDSET, THE POWER THAT DRIVES US TOWARDS THE LOWER DIMENSIONS] *is* enmity against God: for it is not subject to the law of God, neither indeed can be [IT LIES AT A RIGHT ANGLE TO THE KINGDOM OF GOD].
>
> "So then they that are in the flesh cannot please God" (Romans 8:5-8).

> **The spiritual world runs counter to the natural world.**

Understanding is greatly increased here. In the second dimension understanding is limited to seeing the picture as a puzzle (plane). You understand how all the pieces fit together. In the third, understanding is moved up to the level of a Rubik's Cube. In the fourth, understanding encompasses processes, motions, and cycles. Understanding includes movement.

The third dimension has mechanical inventions. The fourth has inventions of power. The third has tools to help you accomplish a task. The fourth has machinery which performs the task. Although the machines may appear stationary, yet they are in high motion. The engine block may be stationary but inside the engine there is power being harnessed.

A better example may be electricity. The wires are stationary but the electricity is moving through the wires at the speed of light. In a sense, the third dimension is about the Industrial Revolution. The fourth is about the Technological Revolution or the Computer Age.

Transcending Time and Space

The time equivalent is no longer limited to a measurable increment. It goes beyond the personal life of the individual. In fact, it goes beyond this temporal life altogether. Here we find the beginnings of eternity.

In pagan terms, this encompasses past lives, the present life, and future lives. In Christianity, we are not shackled with such terms. We have been liberated from such faulty concepts that introduce false hopes and strip us of real hope. We can see more clearly because we have the Word of God as a lamp to our feet and as a light to our path. We have the True Light of the world. We see it simply as eternity past, time, and eternity future.

As the spirit world begins, the pagans use such terms as the aura of man or the inner self. In Christianity, we understand these concepts better as the soul and spirit of man. The spirit world begins in this dimension.

Space in the fourth dimension is greatly expanded over the third dimension. Instead of seeing nations and cities as individual entities, we see the world as a whole. In this realm, divisions lose their significance. It is no longer simply about "my city" or "my nation." Rather, it is about the whole world.

In viewing the symphony, we now find that the musicians are all working together to form a greater sound and progression in music. Though they may all have different instruments they are still playing together. They may even be playing at different times but they are still playing together. Some who have the same instruments may be playing different notes. They are not competing for individual attention. There is a greater goal in mind here. They are working together under the direction of the director. They are producing harmony.

The key word here is "unity." In the secular world this would be evidenced by corporate mergers and cities uniting to form a larger metropolis. Local economies mesh into a global economy. Separate currencies of the third dimension are exchanged for a uniform currency. Governments begin uniting to form coalitions. On a larger scale it becomes nations clamoring for a one world government. Religious bodies start striving for a one world religion.

Boundaries lose their prominence. Borders lose their weight. We are all now interdependent. We can hardly make it without the rest of the world. What happens in Asia affects the financial markets in New York. What happens on Wall Street affects Main Street.

Classes of people are minimized. Classifications tend to lose their importance. Distinctions are still recognized but are not nearly as important. We recognize that we are all in the same boat. The whole becomes greater than the parts.

In the Christian world and on the righteous end of unity, we find the church uniting to work together to accomplish the Great Commission. It is no longer "my church, my ministry, and my organization" but now it becomes "the body of Christ" working together.

> **The key word here is "unity," which brings wholeness.**

Concerning the early church it is written, "they were all with one accord in one place" (Acts 2:1). As a result, they saw something happen that had never happened before. The gift of the Holy Ghost was poured out, first on one hundred twenty, then on an additional three thousand.

The unity of the early church was further demonstrated in Acts 4. "Now the multitude of those who believed were of one heart and one soul; neither did anyone say that any of the things he possessed was his own, but they had all things common" (Acts 4:32, NKJV).

Since the church is the body of Christ and a body must be unified to work properly, Paul called for the church to strive for this unity.

"I, therefore, the prisoner of the Lord, beseech you to walk worthy of the calling with which you were called,

"with all lowliness and gentleness, with longsuffering, bearing with one another in love,

"**endeavoring to keep the unity of the Spirit in the bond of peace**" (Ephesians 4:1-3, NKJV).

The great revival that has been happening in recent years in the nation of Ethiopia has had unity as a trademark of the church there. Brother Teklemariam (their leader) has remarked that whereas we preach revival here in the United States, in Ethiopia they preach unity in the truth. When a church breaks into apostolic revival (especially on a sustained basis), strong unity is manifested.

The Rhythm of Life

In viewing a parade, the fourth dimensional mind would be able to see the whole parade moving in fluid motion. It would not simply be there as a picture that we can view. The parade would be in the process of marching from beginning to end to reach its destination. Here we see the parade in progress. It unfolds before us.

If we tap into the fourth dimension, we will find that there is a rhythm to life. As a young man fresh out of Bible school I heard the noted preacher and thinker J. T. Pugh make the comment how almost thirty years beforehand he had learned about the rhythm of life. If you will learn to tap into the rhythm of life you will find success in your endeavors.

You can find fame, riches, popularity, love -- whatever you desire. It can all be found if you are flowing with the rhythm of life. If you move in stride with the ebb and flow of life, great things beat a path to

> *You can find whatever you desire out of life if you are moving with the rhythm of life.*

your door. To find success you simply swim with the current moving with the rhythm of life. Ride the wave and you will easily arrive with these blessings. The third dimension will simply reflect the fourth dimension. This can be seen in the political world, in economics, in culture, and in individuals' lives.

Part of the sensation we receive while listening to music comes from its relationship to a rhythm. There is great power in rhythm. Life has been tied to rhythm. The heart beats to send the flow of blood to the body in a steady, rhythmic pulse.

A marching army will break step when crossing a bridge because of the power of rhythm. With all of their soldiers marching in perfect rhythm, they could cause the bridge to collapse. There is great power in rhythm. You can find what you think you are looking for if you move with the rhythm of life.

Just as the tide goes out to sea and comes in to shore with a steady rhythm, so life runs its cycles in a steady rhythm. "To every *thing there is* a season, and a time to every purpose under the heaven" (Ecclesiastes 3:1). Just as the earth

> *The third dimension will naturally reflect the fourth dimension.*

rotates to give us the consistent sequence of night and day, so there are times of success. The various seasons of life come to all of us. To make the most of it, all you need to do is to ride the waves when they come.

Strength and health are gained through the proper use of rhythms. Muscles become stronger not just by contracting nor just by relaxing but by both contracting and relaxing. It takes work and rest for the body to be in optimum health. It takes both the intake of food and the release of wastes. The body must inhale and exhale. The natural world is a reflection of the spiritual world. The third dimension will reflect what is found in the fourth dimension.

As we live we do engage in a rhythm of a kind. We sometimes call them habits. We sleep for a time and then we rise for a time. We live in our cycles or with habits. To run against the rhythm of life can be extremely difficult just as it is difficult to break some habits. Spiritually, we do want to establish certain rhythms to our day. Since habits often refer to a choiceless and effortless action, a better word for it may be disciplines. Such rhythms would include prayer time, study of God's Word, learning, work, etc. And the third dimension will naturally reflect the fourth dimension.

Tuning in to the Fourth Dimension

In this fourth dimension there are no barriers, no borders, no boundaries. This realm knows no limitations in regards to the physical world. In a technological and political sense, our world is trying to push into the fourth dimension. This is the reason for so many moves toward a single global government, economy, currency, and village.

In our present age we have broken down many divisions. Modern means of transportation can carry us to the other side of the world very quickly. What used to take months to travel now takes only hours. Automobiles, trains, and airplanes have made faraway places seem close to home.

Communications have broken down many dividing walls. Accents in speaking a language are losing their sharp distinctiveness. In the United States we are developing a uniform "All-American" accent because of radio, television, telephones, and widespread mobility. Barriers are being broken.

With the push of a few buttons you can be talking to someone on the other side of the nation via telephone. With the click of a mouse you can be online with someone on the other side of the world. You can sit still and catch voices from hundreds of miles away by way of radio. You can lie down and catch pictures of events happening on the other side of the globe via television. You do not have to wait to read the news. You can view it in progress.

This is happening twenty-four hours a day. Radio transmitters are sending out their message on their respective frequencies. Television stations broadcast their pictures through satellite all day long. Right where you sit reading this book, there are thousands of spoken words sending messages all around you. Pictures are currently flying all around you.

You may be sitting in a quiet living room all alone. You may be in a restaurant finishing a meal. You may be out by a stream in a national forest. But there still are thousands of these words

> *Access to the fourth dimension requires a "tuning in."*

being spoken though you cannot hear them. There are thousands of pictures floating around and you cannot even see them. The reason is that you are not tuned in to it.

If you had a radio blaring then you would realize there really are words speeding through the place where you are sitting. You just need to catch the radio waves. If you had a television you could tune in and see that there really are many pictures to behold. It is simply a matter of tuning in to it.

The fourth dimension of life cannot be accessed through the "natural" methods. It requires a tuning in. You do not easily sense spirits unless you are tuned in. The spirit world cannot be accessed by methods of the lower dimensions. It takes a radio to catch the radio waves. It takes a spiritual mind to sense the spiritual world.

In the dimension of knowledge (the third), purpose has to do with the temporal world. Though purpose begins there it is only materialistic in nature. Goals were related to this present life, to what we can see, to the concrete. In the dimension of movement (the fourth), purpose stretches into the eternal. It is no longer only materialistic. It is now spiritual as well.

Hope (as is commonly understood) is found in the fourth dimension. Life is not all concrete. We have now entered into a realm where we can hope for things that are not related to this present age. Hope is a powerful motivator.

Spiritual Fire

Fire is no longer something we fly into without a choice as we do in the first dimension. Yes, we do understand it and respect it as found in the second. We even know how to harness its energy towards profitable ends as in the third. But now we have a greater fire. The fire is no longer physical. It is spiritual.

The physical fire cannot affect the spiritual body. In days gone by, numerous Christians were burned at the stake for their faith. But the fire could not harm the more important body -- their spiritual body.

In the fourth dimension and higher (the spiritual world), the fire that threatens is no longer physical but spiritual. If we have not followed the plan of God, then the fire is destructive to us. If we follow God's laws, the fire cannot harm us. If we do not get rid of carnal things that interfere with our walk with God, the fire ever burns us. Jesus referred to a fire that "is not quenched" (Mark 9:43-48).

On the other hand, if our hearts are right, the fire can be a positive thing. It can be used to refine, cleanse, and purify us. Once the prophet Jeremiah had caught hold of this realm, he said that he could not be silent concerning the name of God or His word. It was "in mine heart as a burning fire shut up in my bones" (Jeremiah 20:9).

John the Baptist preached about the coming Messiah. He said,

> "I indeed baptize you with water unto repentance: but He that cometh after me is mightier than I, whose shoes I am not worthy to bear: He shall baptize you with the Holy Ghost, and *with* fire" (Matthew 3:11).

When the Holy Ghost was first poured out, the Bible says, "there appeared unto them cloven tongues like as of fire, and it sat upon each of them" (Acts 2:3). We have a greater fire here than in the natural world.

The fourth dimension has to do with the stimulation of the spirit.

In the fourth, we come into contact with high concepts. These higher concepts are not necessarily tied to education. They include (but are not limited to) faith, hope, love, and wisdom (differentiated from knowledge). This is the place of the great works of the arts. Here are the arts in their highest form. This is appropriate since music, in order for it to be "music," is always in motion. The fourth dimension is a dimension of motion.

Medical science (though mostly a third dimensional knowledge) is sometimes able to reach into the fourth dimension. Perhaps this is why we refer to it as a "practice." It is in motion. In the fourth dimension we are able to tap into the value of rhythm, the rhythm of life.

The first dimension has to do with the stimulation of the senses. The second dimension has to do with the stimulation of the emotions. The third dimension has to do with the stimulation of the mind. The fourth dimension has to do with the stimulation of the spirit. This is the arena of ideas, the battleground for varying philosophies. We have higher concepts in the fourth.

But mixed in with some of these greater ideas are the will, the plan, and the works of Satan. His desire is manifested in this realm. This is where you will find what Satan desires to do. Here is where we do battle with the enemy. This is where we have dreams from the spirit world.

It was here that I learned of Satan's plan for the lives of some people I know. Just last night God revealed to me a particular spirit that was beginning to get into someone's life. They did not tell me anything along these lines at any point beforehand but God revealed it. He revealed it so that I would know how to pray.

The fourth dimension is where we find the beginning of the spiritual world. In this realm there is always motion. Everything is moving. Everything is in progress. This is why when we begin to pray, we have thoughts of every kind coming to our minds. We remember all types of things we have to do. We see it all in our minds. Every conceivable thought vies for our attention.

But we must bring every thought into captivity to the obedience of Christ (II Corinthians 10:5). We are attempting to make contact with the spirit world. We are breaking beyond the third dimension. Everything is in motion.

This constant movement can make for a lot of confusion. Angels and demons both operate in this realm. With all the movement, confusion easily takes control. We do not see clearly in this realm. We only see through a glass darkly. Paul said that there are "so many kinds of voices in the world, and none of them *is* without signification" (I Corinthians 14:10). The gift of discerning of spirits becomes invaluable at this point.

Spiritual Dreams

We have stated that the spiritual world begins in the fourth dimension. Dreams and visions are found in this realm. They can come from God and they may be from the devil. Of course, they may also be from our own human spirits. It can be easy to get confused. We must guard against being deceived.

That is why God gave us His Word -- to help us know when He is speaking and when it is some other spirit. The gift of discerning of spirits helps us as well. The Apostle John told us to verify the origin of the spirits that come our way. "Beloved, do not believe every spirit, but test the spirits, whether they are of God; because many false prophets are gone into the world" (I John 4:1, NKJV). Not everything in the fourth dimension is from God because not every spirit is from God. We must try the spirits according to God's Word to find out their identity or source.

God has always spoken to people in visions and dreams. The Bible records numerous examples of this. He did this with many of the prophets (Daniel 2:19, 7:1-2, Obadiah 1:1, Nahum 1:1). The Lord spoke to Abraham this way according to Genesis 15:1. He spoke to Jacob in dreams (Genesis 31:9-13). Jacob also saw the ladder between heaven and earth in a dream (Genesis 28:12).

His son, Joseph not only had dreams from God but also had a gift in interpreting them (Genesis 37:5, 9, 40:5-22, 41:1-32). Among those for whom he interpreted dreams were the butler and the baker of Pharaoh's court (Genesis 40:5) and the Pharaoh of Egypt (Genesis 41:1). This shows that God spoke not only to His own people through dreams; He also did this with pagans. In this case, it was to show what was in the future.

Sometimes God speaks in dreams to give warnings to people. God warned Abimelech against taking Sarah to be his wife (Genesis 20:3). God warned Laban about how to speak to Jacob (Genesis 31:24). Sometimes God uses dreams to give encouragement and hope. He gave a dream and its interpretation to some Midianite soldiers for Gideon's sake (Judges 7:13-15). The Lord appeared to Solomon in a dream to offer him anything he would ask for (I Kings 3:5). King Nebuchadnezzar had a couple of dreams that were from God (Daniel 2:1, 4:4-18). One dream was given to show the future and the other was given as a warning about his pride.

Dreams did not stop with the Old Testament. The angel of the Lord appeared to Joseph (the stepfather of Jesus) in dreams at least twice. Once it occurred to encourage him to take Mary as his wife (Matthew 1:20). The other time its purpose was to give him direction (Matthew 2:13). The wise men who followed the star at Jesus' birth were warned by God in a dream about which way to take their journey home (Matthew 2:12).

It was even expected that the Lord would speak to people through dreams. The Lord told Moses, Aaron, and Miriam, "If there be a prophet among you, *I* the LORD will make myself known unto him in a vision, *and* will speak unto him in a dream" (Numbers 12:6). When Saul was trying to find an answer from the Lord he became frustrated because the Lord would not answer him, not even through dreams (I Samuel 28:6, 15).

> "God speaketh once, yea twice *yet man* perceiveth it not.
> "In a dream, in a vision of the night, when deep sleep falleth upon men, in slumberings upon the bed;
> "Then he openeth the ears of men, and sealeth their instruction,
> "That he may withdraw man *from his* [MAN'S] purpose, and hide pride from man.
> "He keepeth back his soul from the pit, and his life from perishing by the sword" (Job 33:14-18).

God speaks to men to help man turn from his own way and to follow God's way. Man's way may seem right but the end of it are the ways of death and destruction (Proverbs 16:25). The way of man cannot be found in himself (Jeremiah 10:23). His own direction is marred. He needs to find the Way (John 14:6) that leads to life (Matthew 7:13-14).

Yet not all dreams come from God. This fourth dimension is only the beginning of the spirit world. Both angels and demons can work in this realm. Therefore there can be a lot of confusion. Everything is in motion, both good and evil. There are dreams that have their origin in God. There are dreams that have their origin in a demonic spirit. Arcovio has said, "If you have a dream from God, you will probably eventually have a dream influenced by the enemy."[2] This is because dreams are an entrance to the spiritual world, both righteous and unrighteous.

There are also dreams that have their origin in our own human spirit. These may be dreams which reveal things to us about ourselves. There are dreams which we cause to be dreamed because of the condition of our hearts (Jeremiah 29:8). These dreams will give the appearance of being from God but they are full of deception (Jeremiah 23:26, 17:9).

---

[2] John Arcovio, *Discerning the Spirits of this End Time Apostolic Age* (Stockton, CA: Spirit Led Publications, 1998), 14-15.

And then there are dreams that come as the result of our busy days (Ecclesiastes 5:3, 7). This may be the result of turmoil or confusion in our spirit. Sometimes the dream is full of emptiness. When this is the case, they may easily be dismissed as unimportant. In spite of this, some dreams do come from the spirit world and carry great weight.

Prove Those Spirits

The operation of the gifts of the Spirit starts in this realm of the fourth dimension. So also do those that practice witchcraft. People who have "extra sensory perception" (ESP) operate in this realm. Psychics operate in this realm. They pick up the vibrations that are being transmitted. They tune in to the words and pictures that are in motion in the spiritual world.

Many have thought that they were hearing from God when they were actually hearing from some other spirit. So they went out into the world to give their message but they went out as a "false prophet" according to the Apostle John (I John 4:1). If you learn to try the spirits you can save yourself the disappointment, the pain, and the destruction that comes as a result of believing a demonic spirit.

I was preaching in Arizona where a lady from a "mainline" evangelical Christian church came with a friend to visit a service. Actually, the visitor was one of her church's Sunday School teachers. It so happened on this particular night that I preached about being led of the Spirit. Being a spiritual woman this really impressed her.

She wanted to speak with me after the service. During the course of the conversation she told me that she had indeed received the gift of the Holy Ghost and that God used her in the gifts of the spirit that I referred to.

Normally when someone tells me they have received the Holy Ghost I tend to believe them. But in this case, my spirit did not witness this with her. So I pressed further with questions about her experience.

She told me that she had indeed "spoken with tongues." Still, something did not sit right with me. It turned out her version of speaking with tongues had nothing to do with the language she spoke in prayer while being led of God's Spirit. It had something to do with just loving people and doing good. That was her version of speaking with other tongues.

As I spoke further with her, I found out that her version of operating in the gifts of the Spirit was equally off base. What she actually was involved in was psychic activity. It had nothing to do with hearing the voice of God. She was involved in witchcraft. Her church had brainwashed her into thinking that New Age philosophy was the gospel of Jesus Christ.

I tried in the gentlest and wisest way I knew to tell her there was something greater than what she had. She had indeed made contact with the spirit world. But because she was not taught to try the spirits and because she did not have a foundation of truth in scripture, she was being led down a path that was going to destroy her. Scripture teaches us, "There is a way which seemeth right unto a man, but the end thereof *are* the ways of death" (Proverbs 14:12).

It is not enough simply to establish a foundation of morality and think that you have fulfilled the laws of God. It is not enough to mentally believe a doctrine. We have great promises that we must inherit through faith and patience (Hebrews 6:12).

In talking about some of the great promises we have from God, Paul said, "Therefore, having these promises, beloved, let us cleanse ourselves from all filthiness of the flesh and spirit, perfecting holiness in the fear of God" (I Corinthians 7:1, NKJV). The filthiness of the flesh is found in the first three dimensions. The filthiness of the spirit is located in the fourth dimension.

Spiritual Warfare

Prayer in this realm goes beyond that which affects only this temporary world. Here prayer begins to affect eternity, the spirit realm. Prayer is no longer a complaining session as it can be in the third dimension. It goes beyond seeking to fulfill fleshly needs or carnal desires (lower levels of prayer). It now surpasses simple devotion and thanksgiving. It now enters spiritual warfare.

Prayer in this realm can often be rhythmic or in a singsong manner. Prayer is very much in "motion." Prayer is "dependant" on its momentum. This is because the fourth dimension is one of motion.

The manner of a Christian's warfare is not battle in a physical manner. Our greatest battles are in the fourth dimension and onward. Paul said, "We wrestle not against flesh and blood, but against principalities, against powers, against the rulers of the darkness of this world, against spiritual wickedness in high *places*" (Ephesians 6:12). The New King James Version has those last two words as "the heavenly *places*." Our battles are in the spiritual dimensions.

> "For though we walk in the flesh, we do not war according to the flesh.
> "For the weapons of our warfare *are* not carnal [OF THE FLESH] but mighty [IMPACT-MAKING] in God for pulling down strongholds,
> "casting down arguments and every high thing that exalts itself against the knowledge of God, bringing every thought into captivity to the obedience of Christ,
> "and being ready to punish all disobedience when your obedience is fulfilled" (II Corinthians 10:3-6, NKJV).

I was preaching in a city in the western United States where the pastor, a very spiritual man, told me an unusual story. While he was praying and studying in his office some months beforehand, a powerful demon appeared to him. Immediately, he felt total fear grab a hold of his spirit. This man of God is not one given to fear. He had had other spiritual experiences with enemy spirits but never had felt fear like he did on this occasion.

The demonic spirit gave him a simple message: "Don't mess with me and I won't mess with you." He was saying that as long as the pastor did not enter spiritual warfare against him, things would go well for him. If he warred in the spirit against the enemy, a great battle would ensue. But if he was willing to settle for less he could coexist with the enemy. He could see small victories and gain material things. Only he would not get to see great revival. He just had to be willing to compromise the will of God. But light cannot abide with darkness. Righteousness cannot have fellowship with unrighteousness.

The pastor took special time over the next week to gain the boldness to rebuke the spirit and command him to leave. But the battle did not end. While I spent some time there, the spirit decided to visit again. Without getting into all of the details, it turned it out this spirit was one of the chief lieutenants of the Prince in the Northwest United States.

So for the next few months we entered into a period of spiritual warfare that was very intense. The strangest of things happened (things which, if recorded here, would not be believed by many). But through the blood of Jesus and prayer we gained a great victory over the next few months. Still, the breakthrough has not happened completely. We have seen but a small measure of the work of God accomplished that He desires to bring to that area of the country.

There truly is a spiritual war that is being waged. We are wrestling against spiritual wickedness in high places. We are also wrestling against principalities – those in authority who are purposed to work iniquity. They are purposed to work their own will rather than the will of God.

"Holy Spirit, help us to unify with the body of Christ. Make us whole from our many infirmities. Help us to tune in to the voice of your spirit, moving in syncopation with the rhythm of your life. Give us a discerning ear to hear your direction that we may war a good warfare, keeping the faith. In Jesus' name."

CHAPTER FOUR

THE FIFTH DIMENSION OF LIFE

I heard a story about an interview with Chuck Yeager, the test pilot who first broke the sound barrier. There had been other attempts to fly faster than sound but no one had succeeded as of yet. When Yeager made up his mind that he would do it, he told those with him this would be the day of the successful attempt.

As he flew his plane at increasing speeds, the plane began to shake. The closer he came to breaking the sound barrier the more violently the plane shook. When he was on the brink of flying faster than the speed of sound, the plane shook so violently it seemed that the whole thing would come apart. But as soon as he broke through the sound barrier, everything became smooth.

Yeager was flying faster than anyone had ever flown before. He was moving quicker than ever – so quickly that everything around him was shaking terribly. Then he increased his speed a little bit and everything came to a calm.

The fifth dimension of life is the realm of peace. It is the dimension of dominion. Since this dimension lies at a "right angle" from the fourth, it is seemingly opposed to it. Whereas in the fourth you find everything is in motion and confusion is rampant, in the fifth everything is stationary and full of peace. It is motionless but not like in the third dimension. It is on a much higher level.

The time equivalent in this realm goes beyond a simple eternity in progress, as we would see it in the fourth. Here we are able to see the end from the beginning. You do not have to wait for the process to unfold. It is already completed. You do not have to observe in which direction things are moving as in the fourth dimension. You need not be afraid of how it will all turn out in the end. In the fifth you already know how it will all turn out.

This removes the presence of uncertainty. Everything is already established. The end has been determined before the beginning started. Therefore, there is peace. Not just a sense of security. Not a temporary feeling of safety. Not being sold on an appearance of things settled. There is perfect tranquility. All things are finished.

Here is true peace. Jesus said, "Peace I leave with you. My peace I give to you; not as the world gives do I give to you. Let not your heart be troubled, neither let it be afraid" (John 14:27, NKJV).

Here we have entered into the secret place of the Most High. Therefore, we can abide under the shadow of the Almighty (Psalm 91:1). We possess true security. Therefore, we live in total peace.

The Completed Plan

In viewing the parade, you now see it from a helicopter's point of view. You can see the end of the parade, the middle, and the beginning all at the same time. In the fourth dimension you see the parade as it progresses. But here you see it from a higher level. This is the level of prophecy.

In the fifth dimension is where we find the blueprints for life. This is where we find the completed plans for what is being worked out in the process or motion of the fourth dimension. This is where the gift of prophecy (as is commonly understood) is perfected or completed. This is the dimension of prophecy. This is where we can find the future spelled out.

In the first dimension, you notice the flute. In the second you notice the musician. In the third you notice the various segments of the different bands and parade. In the fourth you hear the progression of the music being played. You hear the symphony play at the direction of the director. You see everyone marching. The parade is in progress. There is constant motion.

In the fifth you have the music already composed. You know how the music is supposed to end because you already have it written on paper. You see the completed work in the composition. The musicians are simply playing out their part. But the work is finished. All that is left is for it to be played out in the fourth dimension. In the fifth dimension you know how the parade will end. You know its destination. It is already planned and written on paper.

In the first dimension you notice the tool. In the second you notice the workman. In the third you notice the whole construction scene with the various divisions of time and place. In the fourth you notice all the activity of the workers running around and building the structure. In the fifth you look at the blueprints. You already can see the completed work.

Here you know how the building will turn out when the fourth dimension is finished. Everything is already settled. Before the fourth dimension starts its activity the fifth dimension has the results established. You can see the end from the beginning. There is no need for worry, panic, or fretting. Everything has already been determined. Here is true peace.

> **Everything is orchestrated from the fifth dimension.**

Whereas in the fourth dimension we found the beginning of eternal purpose being worked out, in the fifth we see total purpose finished. Here we find the cause of the purpose that is being worked out in the fourth.

In the fourth we see the men constructing the building. They have a purpose for their work, their motion. In the fifth we find the cause of their purpose anchored in the blueprints.

In the fourth we see the musicians playing with a purpose. In the fifth we see the reason for their purpose in the composition.

In the fourth dimension we are in warfare. We war against the will, desire, and works of Satan. In the fifth we have the revealed will of God.

The fifth dimension is the storage place for the Blueprints of all blueprints. Here we find the Song of all songs. This is the storehouse for the Pattern of all patterns. The Formula of all formulas is found here. Everything is orchestrated from this dimension.

When we plant a seed, we already know what it will be when it is fulfilled. A corn seed will produce a corn crop. A watermelon seed will produce a watermelon crop. The plan is already complete within the DNA of the seed. Anything that happens to the plant will not change the fruit. It does not matter the type of weather it endures or the kind of soil. The fruit is already determined. The process of growth is only bringing to us what was already written within the code of the seed. Time is only fulfilling what has already been determined -- the harvest of a particular crop.

All of the "formulas" of the operation of faith and the working of the miraculous are found here in the fifth dimension.

The enemy cannot stop us here. This is where we find spiritual dominion. Here, there is no longer a rising up against us. There is no argument against the completed plan. You cannot change it. Everything has already been determined.

In the fourth dimension eternity is in motion. In the fifth it is complete. Actually, we could say that the fourth dimension is the channel to bring to us what is found as complete in the fifth. The third dimension reflects the fourth. The fourth dimension works out in process the plan found in the fifth.

Scripture refers to certain time limitations based on the blueprints of life. Daniel referred to appointed times (Daniel 11:27, 35, 36). In Romans 11:25, Paul refers to "the fulness of the Gentiles." Galatians 4:4 refers to "when the fulness of the time was come." This refers to God's eternal plan. The time was already established. Only the fourth dimension had to play out its part.

God already knew what He was doing. It was all under control. It still is all under control. And it is under God's control. Paul told the Athenians that God "has made from one blood every nation of men to dwell on all the face of the earth, and has **determined their preappointed times** and the boundaries of their dwellings" (Acts 17:26, NKJV).

The angel told the prophet Daniel that certain things would not be able to be understood for a certain time. The angel said, "Go thy way, Daniel: for the words *are* closed up and sealed till the time of the end" (Daniel 12:9).

We all have a time that is appointed to us. It is not that we have no control over how long we have. It is only that the time is limited. We have a promise of long life on the earth if we honor our father and mother (Ephesians 6:1-3). If we live violently and deceitfully we will cut our days short (Psalm 55:23). If we take care of our bodies we may lengthen our years a little bit (Psalm 90:10).

Yet we are still limited by time as long as we are in this earthly body. Hebrews 9:27 says, "It is appointed unto men once to die, but after this the judgment." In this time there will be good days and bad days. But it is all under control, managed by our Creator. The times have already been measured.

Psalm 37:19 tells us that the upright "shall not be ashamed in the evil time." The evil time may come but the upright will not be ashamed. For those that consider the poor, David said "the LORD will deliver him in time of trouble" (Psalm 41:1). In another psalmist's prayer to the Lord, he said, "Remember how short my time is" (Psalm 89:47).

Divided Times

Solomon recognized the powers of the fifth dimension. He understood how certain times are appointed to man. He wrote, "To every *thing there is* a season, and a time to every purpose under the heaven." Heaven refers to the spiritual world. In our temporal world, time is granted for every purpose to be worked out. It seems that every spirit has its day.

"A time to be born, and a time to die; a time to plant, and a time to pluck up *that which is* planted;

"A time to kill, and a time to heal; a time to break down, and a time to build up;

"A time to weep, and a time to laugh; a time to mourn, and a time to dance;

"A time to cast away stones, and a time to gather stones together; a time to embrace, and a time to refrain from embracing;

"A time to get, and a time to lose; a time to keep, and a time to cast away;

"A time to rend, and a time to sew; a time to keep silence, and a time to speak;

"A time to love, and a time to hate; a time of war, and a time of peace" (Ecclesiastes 3:1-8).

In our lives there will be good days and "bad" days. There will be times when we experience gain and other times when we experience loss. There will be times when we are "up" and times when we are "down." There will be times when we feel great and times when we are not feeling so hot.

Solomon said that God "has made everything beautiful in its time" (Ecclesiastes 3:11). There has been a proper place or time appointed for every purpose. This means that even those things that seem bad or painful have an appointed time. "Well," you might say, "it is awfully cruel of a God who is supposed to be so loving to appoint such a bad time for me."

First we must understand that the evil of our situation is not what God has intended for us as the final plan. Many things have been determined but God has determined that everything will be beautiful in its time. In God's plan everything is designed to produce beauty. An artist may have warm colors mixed in with the cool colors in his painting. But they are both designed to enhance the painting.

However, there is a key in all of this. If you have a right heart it will turn every negative event into a positive result. The Apostle Paul wrote, "We know that all things work together for good to them that love God, to them who are the called according to *his* purpose" (Romans 8:28).

If you are called according to His purpose and you love God, all things will work out for your good. It matters not how wrong,

> *If the bad situations do not turn out for our good, then we need to take another look at the condition of our hearts.*

painful, or unjust the present situation may be, it will work out for our benefit. But the key in all of this is to have a right heart. You must love God.

Loving Him is not simply saying that you do. Your actions must proclaim it. Jesus said, "If you love me, keep my commandments" (John 14:15, NKJV). God has appointed all things to have their time and their season because He wants to prove the hearts of men.

"I the LORD search the heart, *I* try the reins [THE MIND OR THE MOST SECRET PARTS, THE THING THAT DETERMINES THE DIRECTION OF MAN], even to give every man according to his ways, *and* according to the fruit of his doings" (Jeremiah 17:10).

David told Solomon to know his God and to

"Serve Him with a loyal heart and with a willing mind; for the LORD searches all hearts and understands all the intent of the thoughts. If you seek Him, He will be found by you; but if you forsake Him, He will cast you off forever" (I Chronicles 28:9, NKJV).

In Revelation 2:23, Jesus identified Himself as "He which searcheth the reins and the hearts." God weighs the hearts of men in scales or balances to prove those hearts that are right towards Him and those that are perverse.

David, who was a man after God's own heart, prayed,

"Search me, O God, and know my heart: try me, and know my thoughts:

"And see if *there be any* wicked way in me, and lead me in the way everlasting" (Psalm 139:23-24).

The higher you rise in the spirit, the purer your spirit must become. The greater the dimension of life and power, the purer your heart, motives, and desires must be. The higher you rise in life, the more is required of you. "Unto whomsoever much is given, of him shall be much required" (Luke 12:48). More is expected from the CEO or the pastor than is expected from the janitor. And God understands the principle that says, "He that is faithful in that which is least is faithful also in much" (Luke 16:10).

> *The higher you rise in the spirit, the purer your spirit must become.*

Witches, warlocks, psychics, and others have tapped into the spiritual world though they have not done so according to the Word of God. They have climbed into the fourth dimension but they have not done so with a right heart. Jesus said, "He that entereth not by the door into the sheepfold, but climbeth up some other way, the same is a thief and a robber.... I am the door: by me if any man enter in, he shall be saved" (John 10:1, 9).

Even so, they recognize a measure of the need for a clean (unhindered) mind. In their circles, if someone is using witchcraft on a very low level, they may use mind-altering drugs to accompany them. But if they desire to rise higher in their powers, they will abstain from using those drugs. They need a clear mind.

If there is any truth to this in witchcraft circles, it is definitely more so with God. The higher you rise the purer you must become. The reason why some folks look up to certain individuals as being men of God or great individuals when they are not even Christian is because the sense a purity in their lives. The purity they sensed was there because that individual was operating in the fourth dimension.

If you love God and are called according to His purpose (rather than walking according to your own purpose), you know that every event will work out in your favor. This gives you great peace of mind. No matter how bad it seems, it will still work out for my good as long as I love God. Things may not be okay right now but I know that they will be all right. All that is needed is to be in perfect alignment with His purpose, His will.

Complete Alignment

There is perfect peace when you are in perfect alignment with the laws of the spirit. In the fourth dimension you will find the best of the arts -- great music, great paintings, great writings, etc. In the fifth dimension you will find genius.

True genius is being in perfect alignment with the laws of the spirit. Men as Sir Isaac Newton and Albert Einstein are considered among the greatest of all geniuses. They were able to find the laws that govern the entire natural world. The laws of the fifth dimension govern the powers, the motions, and the processes of the fourth dimension.

There have been many geniuses that have been converted to Christianity simply from coming into contact with the manifested plan of God found in the fifth dimension. Astronomers who were once atheists have been converted after coming into contact with hidden codes in galaxies that testify of the Creator. Mathematicians who were once atheists have been converted once they rose so high in their learning of mathematics that they began to find the plan of the Creator. Experts of every type have found God's witness in creation.

This is why Paul said that mankind was without excuse (Romans 1:20). There is a level of learning where, if you are honest with yourself, you will begin to come to the knowledge of the truth. You will begin to see the plan of God. This is not to say that you can find God with your intellect. It is only to say that if you have a right heart, you will find God's witness when you come into alignment with His world.

Being in perfect alignment has to do with placing everything in its proper position. It is truth in balance. When the wheels of a car are aligned, they must be put

> *Perfect alignment has to do with placing everything in its proper position.*

into their proper place with relation to the rest of the car. The wheels must be made to work together properly. The wheels must not work separately, each with a mind of its own. It must be made to work as one.

When you know how the laws of life work, how the system operates, and you are in alignment with it, you will have perfect unity. You will have great peace. You come into contact with God, with His eternal plan. You minimize the friction. You minimize the bad moods, the rotten attitudes, and the selfish mindset. You remove the bitterness, envy, and jealousies. You eliminate uncertainty and worrying.

> **Spiritual alignment has to do with a right spirit.**

Prayer puts us in perfect alignment with the plan of God. When we study God's Word we understand the proper place of all things. It is our Blueprint. When we line up with it we place ourselves in alignment with the laws of God and His kingdom.

Alignment in the spirit has to do with inward things, the matters of the heart. This is why an attitude of repentance is so important. A right spirit is necessary for perfect alignment in the spirit. A clean heart is vital to perfect alignment. Everything can then be set in order, in its proper place. But we need a right heart (more on spiritual alignment in Part II).

Peaceful Dominion

Jesus spoke of serving God and God alone in Matthew 6:24. Then He said,

> "...Do not worry about your life, what you will eat or what you will drink; nor about your body, what you will put on. Is not life more than food and the body more than clothing?
>
> "Look at the birds of the air, for they neither sow nor reap nor gather into barns; yet your heavenly Father feeds them. Are you not of more value than they?
>
> "Which of you by worrying can add one cubit to his stature?
>
> "So why do you worry about the clothing? Consider the lilies of the field, how they grow: they neither toil nor spin;
>
> "and yet I say to you that even Solomon in all his glory was not arrayed like one of these.
>
> "Now if God so clothes the grass of the field, which today is, and tomorrow is thrown into the oven, *will He* not much more *clothe* you, O you of little faith?
>
> "...But seek first the kingdom of God and His righteousness, and all these things shall be added to you" (Matthew 6:25-30, 33, NKJV).

The bird does not worry whether or not he can find food. He just believes that he will find it if he goes out looking. He is in alignment with his world.

The lily is not worried that she may not be able to produce the beauty required of her. She simply lives -- and the beauty comes out. She grows -- and the splendor unfolds. This is because she is in perfect alignment with her world. She is effortlessly playing her part. The beauty has already been determined. It only needs to be worked out according to the plan.

If man would get in perfect alignment with his world (with his purpose and God's will for him) he would not live in fear about his basic necessities. The bird is not worried. The lily is not afraid. All that is necessary concerning us is to live according to the pattern that has been determined for us.

Praying in the Fifth Dimension

From his high place in the mountains, the eagle decides it is time to evacuate from his place of comfort. He lifts his head, spreads his wings and with the grace of a ballerina begins to fly. He escapes from his place of security. Yet, he has not lost his sense of security. He is not worried about falling. He is not scared of the heights. He has a peace about this.

He knows instinctively that everything normally falls to the earth unless it is either resting on something or hanging on something. Still he is not afraid to suspend himself in the air. He is not fearful to throw himself to that which he cannot see. He gives himself to the wind for he knows that he is subscribing to a higher law. He knows how to fly. He is in alignment with his world. So he is at home though he is suspended between heaven and earth.

He does not need to worry about flapping his wings wildly. He is proficient in the air. He hardly even moves. He has mastered the movements of the wind. He does not live beneath the wind. He rises above it. The wind becomes his tool. Any wind that blows will work to his benefit. He is in a "higher realm."

When we are in alignment we will not have to worry about flapping our wings wildly. We will not run in an endless circle of frantic prayer and spiritual activity hoping to accomplish the impossible. We are at perfect peace. And the impossible comes knocking on our door.

Spiritual music is often beneficial in helping us pray. If it is truly spiritual (in quality as opposed to style or category) its thoughts and motions help propel us into the fourth dimension. But in the fifth dimension music is no longer a tool that helps us. We have surpassed motion to come into contact with the completed plan, with the laws of the spirit.

Saul needed the skilful playing of a musician anointed by God to give him relief from the demonic spirits in the fourth dimension who plagued him. He found that musician in David. What set David apart from other musicians was not that he was only a skillful musician but that the LORD was with him (I Samuel 16:14-19).

Elisha was once called upon to give a word from the LORD to the kings of Israel and Judah. Before he prophesied on this particular occasion, he asked for someone to play a minstrel. Then the hand of the LORD came on him and he began to prophesy. The music was able to help Elisha tap into the spiritual world to give the kings direction (II Kings 3:15).

> *Prayer in this realm takes on a prophetic element.*

Oftentimes in service we will do the same thing. We spend some time in worship, prayer, and praise using music as a tool to help usher us into the presence of God. Once we are safely into the moving of the Spirit of the Lord, then we normally have the preacher give us the Word from God. We used the anointed music of the fourth dimension to get us in the right frame of mind to hear the plan of God.

Prayer in the fifth dimension ceases from being a worry session. There is no room for fear. Praying in this realm includes the hearing of the voice of God very clearly. The still small voice is heard with clarity.

Prayer in this realm takes on a prophetic element. You now call for things to line up to the eternal plan of God. We pray "in Christ's stead, be ye reconciled to God" (II Corinthians 5:20). We pray, "Not my will, but thine, be done" (Luke 22:42).

You are able to call those things which are not as though they were. You are walking in the image of God. You find it in the plan of God and call for it to take place. The impossible is then made into reality.

How does God do this? "Before they spring forth I tell you of them" (Isaiah 42:9). God tells us what will be. Then we speak the word which God has given us and God brings it to pass. "Surely the Lord GOD will do nothing, but he revealeth His secret unto His servants the prophets" (Amos 3:7). Why would God do this? God does this because He is a "revealer of secrets" (Daniel 2:47).

"Lord, lift us up where we belong, where the eagles fly over the mountain high."

The musician need not worry how the symphony will sound -- if he will play his part according to the composition. The worker need not be concerned how the building will turn out -- if he will do his part according to the blueprint. They only need to get in alignment with what has already been determined.

So we need not worry about the insignificant details of our lives if we will seek first the Kingdom of God and His righteousness. When we find the laws of the kingdom of God and get in alignment with them, all the things we may need will be added to us. If we will diligently seek it out and get in alignment with its principles all things will work for our good.

Do you need peace? Bread? Clothing? Healing? A place to rest? Do you need a messy situation to be brought to a calm? Get in alignment with the kingdom of God.

A miracle from the fifth dimension can restore the mind of one who has gone insane. In this dimension everything is brought into alignment with the perfect plan of God. Peace is released to calm a storm.

Everything will turn out fine if we get in line with the perfect will of God. It is designed to turn out wonderfully. Everything is designed to turn out beautifully (Ecclesiastes 3:11). You get the feeling that everything is going to be all right. In fact, you possess a blessed assurance when you know the plan of God.

I have read the back of the book and we win. There is a new heaven and a new earth. A new city is prepared for us. It is a true "city of gold". The street of the city is made of pure gold. Its walls are made of jasper, furnished with precious jewels. Every type of precious stone is found there in abundance.

The glory of God illuminates it. This is why there is no nighttime there. There is no need for fear. Every tear is wiped away. No longer will there be pain, death, sorrow, or crying. Everything is found in absolute perfection.[3]

The promise of peace is not only for our future home. It will work for today. Jesus said,

---

[3] See Revelation 21:1-2, 4, 14, 18-21, 23, 25, 27, 22:2-5.

"Peace I leave with you, my peace I give unto you: not as the world giveth, give I unto you. Let not your heart be troubled, neither let it be afraid.

"...And now I have told you before it come to pass" (John 14:27, 29).

This is true peace, a prophetic peace, a peace of the fifth dimension, a peace that passes all understanding (Philippians 4:7).

"Heavenly Father, purify our hearts. Purify our hearts that we may see you. Create in us a clean heart and a right spirit. Help us to surpass the turbulence of this world and live in your peace. Help us be in alignment with your perfect will. Rather than our will being done, let your will be done in our lives as it is in heaven. Let everything in our lives be orchestrated by you. Grant us dominion over all the plans and works of the enemy. In the name of our wonderful Savior, Jesus Christ."

CHAPTER FIVE

THE HIGHER DIMENSIONS
The Sixth Dimension of Life

The sixth dimension of life is the dimension of pure power and creativity. This contains greater power than all of the lower dimensions combined. Of course, this dimension lies at a "right angle" to the dimension below it. It seems to run counter to it.

In the fifth dimension everything is settled and established. The plan is complete. But the sixth dimension is where the creative plan is written, which is found as already established in the fifth. This is the place where the writing or the framing of the fifth dimension takes place.

The sixth dimension follows the pattern of the "right angle" in that it seems to conflict with the fifth. It seems to run counter to the perfect peace of the lower dimension. Yet, peace is never interrupted because of the purity found here. The perfected love in this dimension leaves no room for fear to move in.

This dimension is in motion but on a much higher plane than the dimension of motion (fourth). This is the place where you write the blueprints that are found in the fifth dimension which, in turn, provides perfect peace and determines the outcome of the fourth dimension. This is where the energy is framed that settles the fifth realm and is on display in the fourth. The composition that was a finished product in the fifth has been composed here. All things are created in this dimension. This is where you write the fifth dimension. This is the point of beginnings.

The mind behind the plan is found here. The thought behind the word is here. The forces behind the laws are determined here. In this realm creative power is released. Here we find power to create worlds. John said,

"In the beginning was the Word, and the Word was with God, and the Word was God.

"The same was in the beginning with God.

"All things were made by Him; and without Him was not any thing made that was made" (John 1:1-3).

Creative miracles come from this dimension. These are miracles where an arm which has been severed (or perhaps has never grown) begins to grow supernaturally. These miracles give sight to the blind and raise the dead. They can give the retarded a sound mind. It is much like the composer who composes. This is where the engineer designs, the architect draws, and the planner plans. This is where the laws of the universe are framed, spiritual and physical.

> **Creative miracles are found in the sixth dimension.**

Here is where you can supersede the law or the plan of the fifth dimension. You can actually change the things found in the fifth dimension if you are operating in the sixth dimension. Any lower dimension can be changed or superseded by any higher dimension. In this domain you purpose the lower dimensions. This is where you can establish the plan of the fifth dimension that is worked out in the fourth.

Jesus did say, "I will give you the keys of the kingdom of heaven, and whatever you bind on earth will be bound in heaven, and whatever you loose on earth will be loosed in heaven" (Matthew 16:19, NKJV). He did allow man to come in and change the plan of the fifth dimension.

He also said, "If two of you agree on earth concerning anything that they ask, it will be done for them by My Father in heaven" (Matthew 18:19, NKJV). He became even more specific when He said, "If ye shall ask anything in my name, I will do *it*" (John 14:14).

This is where Elijah was when he prophesied to Ahab, "As the LORD God of Israel liveth, before whom I stand, there shall not be dew nor rain these years, **but according to my word**" (I Kings 17:1).

Moses was in this dimension when he "changed" the mind of God (Exodus 32:6-14). The plan of the fifth dimension had determined that the people of Israel would be destroyed in judgement for their corrupted worship. But when Moses interceded, he changed the course of the future. The plan was changed.

This is the place Abraham was trying to reach when he was interceding for Lot and trying to save the cities of Sodom and Gomorrah from destruction.

> *In this realm, there is no selfishness.*

He ended up only being able to save Lot and his two daughters. He almost had Lot's wife but he could not override her will.

In the fifth dimension, everything is settled and established. Courses are unalterable. They are "set in stone." But when you get into the sixth dimension, you realize the plan of the fifth dimension can be changed.

You realize that you were not predestined to an end without a choice or a will. You were not predestined to spend eternity in heaven or hell regardless of your decisions. Jesus said that "God so loved the world, that He gave His only begotten Son, that **whosoever** believeth in Him should not perish, but have everlasting life" (John 3:16). The Apostle Peter quoted the prophet Joel when he said that "**whosoever** shall call on the name of the Lord shall be saved" (Acts 2:21).

Where you live in eternity will be the result of the decisions you make. You were created with a choice. That was determined in the sixth dimension –

> *Faith is unhindered when its motive is an unselfish love.*

a place of pure love, ultimate creativity, and great power.

One would be tempted to think that if they were able to get into this realm, then they could orchestrate all plans to their own advantage. But in this world there is no selfishness. There is only pure love, charity of the highest kind. This is the home of the love of I Corinthians 13.

This dimension is the lace where faith is mixed together perfectly with love. The truth is that faith works by love (Galatians 5:6). Faith is unhindered when its motive is an unselfish love.

When you reach this destination, you are trusted with "power over the nations" (Revelation 2:26). This is because now God knows that you will not use it to serve an unrighteous, selfish purpose that is contrary to the will of God. Power is safest when it is in the hands of the purest.

The gifts of the Spirit have a complete free flow to the greatest degree here in the sixth. In the fourth dimension they may "miss it." It is not perfect. There is only a beginning of the gifts in operation. In the fifth dimension, the gifts can tell what has been established and predetermined. You can write history in advance.

Prophecy in its higher form (its foretelling form) is found in the fifth.

Power is safest when it is in the hands of the purest.

In this realm, prophecy and faith reach a causative form. You speak the words that determine the plan. In this realm, you determine that which will govern the worlds, that which will rule the dimensions beneath it. You have power over the nations.

The Seventh Dimension of Life

The seventh dimension of life is perfect unity with God. We have fellowship and intimate interaction with God's omnipotence, omniscience, and omnipresence. Jesus prayed "that they may be one, as we *are*" (John 17:11). As the firstborn among many brethren (Romans 8:29), Jesus was our example in order that we may follow in His steps (I Peter 2:21)[4]. We are to walk as He walked. We are to be like Him.

Jesus continued in His prayer,

"Neither pray I for these alone, but for them also which shall believe on me through their word;
"That they all may be one; as thou, Father *art* in me, and I in thee, that they also may be one in us....
"And the glory which thou gavest me I have given them; that they may be one, even as we are one:
"I in them, and thou in me, that they may be made perfect [COMPLETE] in one" (John 17:20-23a).

At this point all that we ask is done. All that we speak is perfect (complete) and is accomplished. Our words do not fall to the ground. Jesus said, "If you abide in me, and my words abide in you, you will ask what you desire, and it shall be done for you" (John 15:7, NKJV).

In Revelation Chapters 2 and 3, Jesus had seven messages for the seven churches in what was then known as Asia. At the close of each message He told them two things. One was "He who

---

[4]David Sanzo, *The Key to the Kingdom* (Mobile, AL: Companion Press, 1997), 10-17.

has an ear, let him hear what the Spirit says to the churches"
(Revelation 2:7, 17, 29, 3:6, 13, and 22, NKJV).

The other message was a promise to those that overcame.
The seventh promise to the seventh church talked about overcoming
for the seventh time. Seven is God's number for perfection, for
completion. When we have overcome fully and perfectly, we
receive the promise of the final point of power and authority -- a
seat in the throne of God.

"To him who overcomes I will grant to sit with Me on
My throne, as I also overcame and sat down with My
Father on His throne" (Revelation 3:22, NKJV).

"Lord, lift us up to sit with you in heavenly places in Christ
Jesus." (Ephesians 2:6, 3:7-12).

In conclusion, we find a general outline of the different
levels of life. In relation to the focus of our attention, we can look at
it like this. In the first dimension we are concerned with survival
and physical pleasure. In the second, we are concerned with social
pleasure and any necessary work to accomplish those ends. In the
third, we are concerned with knowledge.

In the fourth we are concerned with high concepts, the
beginning of the spiritual world. In the fifth we find the plan and
the blueprints to life. We have the laws that govern all things. In
the sixth we have pure, unadulterated love and are able to access the
creative power of God. In the seventh we have true unity with God.

The way we view life depends on the dimension that
dominates our lives. A person in the first dimension refers to sexual
activity, drunkenness, the misuse of drugs, or some other pleasure-
seeking or thrill seeking state when he or she speaks of having a life,
"living it up," or "really living." One in the second dimension will
usually refer to a social life when they think of "having a life."

Someone in third dimension will usually have status or
possessions of earthly things or earthly goals in mind. Mention
"having a life" to someone in the fourth dimension and they will
equate it with having a life where you are accomplishing a higher
purpose – purposes that surpass this temporal earth. The fifth
dimensional mind will think of living in accordance with the will of
God. Beyond that, the quality of life becomes so much greater than
what we can possibly imagine in our finite minds. All of this
greatly influences the pursuits that dominate our lives. It affects our
time, our loves, our desires, our very beings.

"Awesome Creator, develop in us a pure heart. Help us to
be free from selfishness. Enable us to love with an unselfish love

that the faith of God may work freely in our lives. Help us to love with a pure love that your creative power may work in and through us. Lift us up to that High place where we can fellowship you -- where we can fellowship Your omnipotence, Your omniscience, and Your omnipresence. Lift us into Your will. Make us one with You. Help us to be one with you. In Jesus' name."

CHAPTER SIX

LOVE IN SEVEN DIMENSIONS

We can apply the principles of the seven dimensions of life to numerous elements of life. For example we could view love in seven dimensions. This will be profitable since faith works by love (Galatians 5:6) and the greater the faith we desire to exercise, the greater love we must demonstrate.

The first dimension of love that man experiences is a selfish love, which is only concerned with satisfying the flesh. It is a love limited to sexual love and a desire for those things or people who can help us fulfill the desires of our flesh. It is a manipulative love for selfish pleasures. It is a love that has been reduced to being trapped to a physical pleasure or a sexual release alone. It is better understood as sexual lust.

The values of this world system would have us to think that all love is sexual love. In reality, all love is not sexual in nature. All love does not need a sexual fulfillment. If we allowed ourselves to degenerate to this first dimensional type of thinking, our love would be shallow indeed. We would be trapped in misery.

The truth is that there are many avenues of fulfillment for love. There is a love that a parent has for a child. But this love is not to find a sexual release. Those who do so not only destroy their own lives but also traumatize the lives of all the children they molest.

When love is forced into a sexual fulfillment alone, it introduces death of some kind -- whether physical, mental, emotional, or spiritual. Physical death is evidenced by diseases of various sorts. Mental or emotional death would include a life trapped by guilt and fear as well as a variety of syndromes and disorders. Spiritual death is separation from God. Therefore, it is separation from true love, joy, peace, and life.

> **The first dimension of love is a manipulative love for selfish purposes.**

There is a love that siblings will have for each other. Again, this is not intended to find a sexual fulfillment. There is a love that two soldiers who have shared a foxhole together in combat will have for each other. It is a loyalty that is truly intense. But sex is not the proper fulfillment for it.

There is a love between two people who have shared a traumatic event in their lives. But this does not mean they have to become sexually involved. There is a love between high school buddies. There is a love between teammates on sports teams. There is a love between co-workers. There is a love between best friends. But, contrary to Hollywood promotions, it does not mean that it must be manifested sexually.

This is a fallacy that many fall into when they adopt this world's idea of love. They think just because they have a love for another person of the opposite sex, that somehow it means they must hop into bed with them. They suppose that just because they share a love for someone who is another person's spouse that they must somehow carry on an affair with them. They assume just because they share a love for someone of the same sex that it must mean they are some type of homosexual and that the love they have for the other person of the same sex must be released in a sexual fashion.

But, as we have seen, there are many different types of love. God has designed it so that only one type of love is to find a sexual fulfillment. That type of fulfillment is only to be found through your husband or wife after marriage.

The second dimension of love is a social love. This love is inclusive of others not just for a manipulative or directly selfish sense but because there is a fulfillment in being loved. We love because we are loved. It is a reactionary love.

Children love their parents because their parents provide for them physically, emotionally, and otherwise. Parents give a sense of security to their children. So the children respond with love for their parents. They desire to please those who provide so much for them.

This love is a reciprocal love. Love on this level is based on a mutual benefit. "I will love you as long as you love me." Friendship is based on a mutual love. "I will be your friend as long as you are mine. We will hang out, have fun together, and otherwise experience life together."

The dog loves his master because his master loves him and takes care of him. The dog loves out of loyalty and a desire for

> *The second dimension of love is a reactionary love.*

friendship. He loves from a desire to play and to have a social relationship. He has an emotional attachment – reactionary love.

The third dimension of love is one that is based more on knowledge than a simple feeling or need. It is based on a commitment of some kind. Here we are no longer just friends when it suits us. We are committed to work through problems that may develop. We love someone and are loyal to them simply based on the knowledge that they are our brother, sister, cousin, etc.

Greater Love

The fourth dimension of love is a united love. Here we bind together because of a common purpose. We unite to reach a common goal. We desire to build a dream together. Since the fourth dimension is a dimension of motion, the fourth dimensional love is a love that is in action. It is not simply a feeling or thought. It is more than knowledge. It needs to express itself. It must do something to help, to show kindness, to communicate.

The fifth dimension of love is a sacrificial love. Here we are not looking for anything to gain necessarily. We are willing to make sacrifices that do not help us but will help someone we love. This is an unselfish love. It is a love for love's sake.

It is also a disciplined love. Here we are willing to suffer rejection from those we love in order to be able to help them in the end. It is love according to a perfect plan. There is an end result in mind, not necessarily a temporary feeling or acceptance by them.

It takes a measure of this level of love for a parent to properly discipline a child for a wrong action, a wrong word, or (most importantly) a wrong attitude. As long as the parent is more interested in being accepted by the child or not incurring the child's wrath, the parent cannot love in the fifth dimension of love. They must be willing to sacrifice not just things but of themselves.

"Greater love hath no man than this, that a man lay down his life for his friends" (John 15:13). The greatest love man gives is to sacrifice his life for a friend. This is a sacrificial love. But this is not to be confused as the greatest love. There is a greater love.

The sixth dimension of love is an unconditional love. The Bible says that Christ died for the ungodly. He died for us while we were yet sinners (Romans 5:6, 8). He did not just lay His life down for friends. He laid it down for His enemies as well. Jesus "is the propitiation for our sins: and not for our's only, but also for *the sins of* the whole world" (I John 2:2). He demonstrated an unconditional love.

> **The sixth dimension of love is an unconditional love.**

Here love is not based simply on whether or not a condition is fulfilled. Love is given totally and unconditionally. It is free love with no strings attached. Here we have perfect love, completed love. It is a greater love than the greatest love humanity can have (unless the love of God flows through you). More than giving your life for a friend, it is being willing to give it for someone who comes far short of being friendly to you.

In a sixth dimensional love, there are no hidden agendas. No secret plans are found. Just genuine love. It is an uncontaminated love. It is a pure love. It is an unselfish love. It has no impurities.

This is the reason why we can write the plans of the fifth dimension. When we are here in the sixth dimension, there are no hidden motives. Love is as pure as it can be. We will make blueprints that are motivated by total love. The love of I Corinthians 13 is rooted here.

"Love suffers long *and* is kind; love does not envy; love does not parade itself, is not puffed up;

"does not behave rudely, does not seek its own, is not provoked, thinks no evil" (I Corinthians 13:4-5, NKJV).

We may be tempted to think that this is the greatest type of love -- unconditional love. But this is not so. Unconditional love is only a sixth dimensional love. Truly how great a love it is. Yet, there is a greater love. The love of God is a greater love. God's love is more than an unconditional love. It is more than a sixth dimensional love. It is a seventh dimensional love.

The seventh dimension of love is an empowering love. This goes beyond simply being unconditional. With unconditional love you love the sinner even in the error of their ways. With empowering love, you are able to change the sinner from the error of their ways. In the sixth dimension, you love them in spite of all their sins, weaknesses, faults, blind spots, and shameful deeds. In the seventh dimension, you can love them with an empowering love. Your love empowers them to change. They no longer remain the same. They do not stay in the same condition.

Your love lifts them. Your love empowers them to rid themselves of the snare into which they have fallen. They are empowered to be free, to be liberated from their bondage. They are now free to grow, to rise higher.

One songwriter wrote,

"I was sinking deep in sin, far from the peaceful shore,
Very deeply stained within, Sinking to rise no more;
But the Master of the sea heard my despairing cry,
From the waters lifted me, now safe am I.

"Love lifted me! Love lifted me!
When nothing else could help, Love lifted me!"[5]

We may refer to this empowering love as the grace of God. It is that amazing grace that saved and changed the wretch we once were. "I was once was lost but now am found. I was blind but now I see." The grace of God, this empowering love, changed us from our previous condition.

The more love you demonstrate, the more value you have as an individual. If you desire to increase your value

> **The seventh dimension of love is an empowering love.**

or worth, demonstrate more love. We are not just talking about any type of love. We are talking about the higher dimensions of love.

If you are worried about your self-esteem, understand that your self-esteem will grow as you learn to rise into the higher dimensions of life. If you desire to exercise faith in the fifth dimension, you will have to love in the fifth dimension. If you desire to pray a fifth dimensional prayer you must love with a fifth dimensional love first.

Many of Jesus' miracles were accomplished because He was "moved with compassion." If we will love on the same level, if we will be moved with His compassion, we can see similar works. If

---

5 "Love Lifted Me" Copyright 1912 by John T. Benson, Jr.

we desire to exercise faith on a sixth dimensional level, we must love on a sixth dimensional level. Since faith works by love (Galatians 5:6), love is our key to exercising greater faith.

"Lord, help us to love like only you can love. Help us to love with the love of God. Help us to love according to your plan. Enable us to love unconditionally. And most of all, help us to love with an empowering love, to love with a love that empowers those around us to be transformed into your image. In the most precious name of Jesus."

CHAPTER SEVEN

THE GARDEN OF EDEN

When God created man and placed him in the Garden of Eden, He made man in His own image, in His own likeness. We were designed to be like Him. Looking at this with an eye to the seven dimensions, we can see that man was made to live on a much higher level of life. This is not just because we "had it made" in the garden but because of the absence of death of any kind.

God made man in a very high spiritual (and physical) state. Adam and Eve did not have trouble learning the will of God. The Bible states that they were able to hear the voice of the LORD God walking in the garden (Genesis 3:8).

Man was probably originally created in the fifth dimension with the will of God being that he eat of the tree of life and rise into the seventh dimension. Scripture tells us that man was made in the image of God. However, it also tells us that man was made a little lower than the angels (Psalm 8:5, Hebrews 2:7). The angels do not live in the seventh dimension for we know that it is God's desire that we some day rise higher than the angels to judge them (I Corinthians 6:3).

God gave man dominion over all the birds, the fish, and every other living thing on earth. Man lived in complete peace. He had full dominion. Dominion and peace are both found at no less than the fifth dimension. There was no room for fear. Adam had authority and power. He could command things to work and they would work with him according to his dominion. He had no sickness or disease that plagued him. He did not struggle with syndromes or disorders. He did not experience death.

They were living in a very high dimension of life. They were not yet at the seventh for sure. They had not yet eaten of the tree of life. Still, they were much higher than man is in his present state.

> **When man fell, he was cut off from a measure of the power of the spirit.**

In the Garden of Eden, God gave man a command. It stated that man was permitted to eat the fruit of every tree in the garden with one exception. He could not eat the fruit of the tree of knowledge of good and evil. If they did eat of this tree, God warned them that they would surely die. Evil can be seen as the search for the captivity of the lower dimensions.

At some point, Satan came into the garden in the form of a serpent and convinced Eve to try the fruit from the forbidden tree. Being deceived, she did as was suggested to her. She then gave some to Adam who ate of it as well. This opened the door to fatal pleasures which produce misery. They had sought to find life by living in the lower dimensions. They decided to learn the knowledge of evil. This opened the door to wickedness. This opened the gate to hell, death, and destruction.

The warning that God had given them beforehand now kicked into gear. They were stripped from living in this higher dimension of life. They fell to lower ways of living. They truly did die in relation to how they were used to living. They were cast out of the Garden of Eden.

Man no longer had full dominion over the earth and every living thing as he had while living in the garden. He could not command things to work and find them working in easy order. He now had to work by the sweat of his face to get things to go his way (Genesis 3:19).

He was cut off from a measure of the power of the spirit. Indeed, he still could see fruit grow but now it required much effort - - the sweat of his face. Thorns and thistles would grow in opposition to man. Demonic spirits could now work against his very spirit and life. There was now a force that was unleashed in his life. This force, this law, this nature became a part of his very being. It drove him towards the lower dimensions. We now refer to it as the carnal nature.

The will of man was now more easily influenced by negative influences (such as fear, suspicion, criticism, and doubt) than it was by positive influences (such as faith, hope, and love). You could still appeal to man to rise higher but his natural tendency was to degenerate. It became easier for humanity to allow a negative mindset to take control. Laziness took the place of dominion, unless they were willing to overthrow that weakness by being willing to work by the sweat of their face.

Instead of being able to rise to higher places with ease, man now had to struggle (usually with himself) to get there. Now it took

> *The will of man was now more easily influenced by negative influences (such as fear, suspicion, criticism, and doubt) than it was by positive influences (such as faith, hope, and love).*

effort (the sweat of his face) to gather his will together to focus on that which was life producing. It became very easy to develop a habit of following the path of least resistance. It has been stated that following the path of least resistance causes both rivers and men to become crooked. It became easy for man to become corrupted. His spirit could easily be twisted away from its original design.

This is why it can be so difficult to make yourself pray. This is why it can be so hard to bring yourself to give, to forgive, to submit to authority, to control the carnal nature, etc. It is the sweat of our face.

Adam and Eve did die that day. They went from their high estate to the lower dimensions. Not only did Adam and Eve know good (how to rise higher and higher in the dimensions of life), they now also knew how to degenerate to the lower dimensions. A doorway was opened that put man on the road to ultimate condemnation. A force was set in motion to drive him toward destruction. The escalator started moving downward to doom. The death trap was sprung.

Yet man was not left without hope. God gave the promise of redemption through their seed. When Jesus came, He opened the way back to life. He came that we might have life and have it more abundantly. We can now rise back into the higher dimensions.

Rebirth

To rise from one dimension to another requires a great willingness to change. When we rise from one dimension to the next, we undergo such a drastic change for the better that we can say we have been born again. In order to change and to rise from one dimension to another we must be willing to die to ourselves, to turn at a "right angle." We must confront the lower level directly, to contradict it and its work.

In order to rise to the higher world we have to die to the lower world. You must be willing to die to death so that you can be alive to life. You must be determined to break the habit of following the path of least resistance.

> *When man fell, he became the slave of that which he was once the master.*

"Except a corn of wheat fall into the ground and die, it abideth alone: but if it die, it bringeth forth much fruit" (John 12:24). The seed has to die to itself in order to live in the greater dimension. The seed has to die to its own world in order to be born again into a higher life. So it is that when we die to the lower worlds, we can be "reborn" in the higher worlds. In order to save our lives we must lose it (Mark 8:34-35). And when we are reborn into a higher world we experience a level of life, joy, love, and peace that we had not known before.

When the child is born, it is not that it gains life at the birthing experience. It was already alive. Only now, since it has died to its old way of living, it rises to a new world. It is born. It has a new level of life.

So it is when we are born again. We rise to a new and greater world. Yes, we were alive before but not like we are now. We are experiencing a greater vibrancy, a greater sense of life.

The reverse is also true. When we fall from a higher dimension to a lower dimension, we can say that a part of us died. Sometimes when someone very dear to us is removed from us we say that a part of us died within us. It may be because we allowed ourselves to fall into a lower dimension. Perhaps they were able to help us live in or reach for a higher dimension. When we lost them, we lost their influence. So we revert to the lower levels of our lives.

When we fall from any dimension to the one beneath it we have backslid to a degree. We may not be totally out in the world but we have slid from the place where we once lived. We have slid backwards. We have gone in the wrong direction. We have gone in the opposite direction that God desires us to go. Instead of going towards greater life, we have meandered towards greater death.

When we talk about man's exodus from the Garden of Eden, we often refer to the "fall of man." This is a properly worded phrase. Man did fall. He fell from his greater state. He opened the door that forced him to continue to decay into the lower dimensions. He opened the door that caused him to die.

Now he had to fight against sickness and disease (Romans 5:12). He developed syndromes and disorders. Now he faced death. He truly did die.

Man now had to wrestle with being trapped in a lower dimension. He had to run up the escalator that is moving downward just to keep in the same place. He had to work by the sweat of his face. He had to work against his fleshly nature, which wants to degenerate into lower dimensions. That condition is death, especially when you know what it is like to live freely in the higher dimensions. Man now had to work underneath his design. He had to live beneath his privilege. He fell from his original creation.

He was now a slave of that which he was once the master. He once ruled over the environment. Now he was subject to it. He once freely ruled over his body. Now it fought against him every step of the way -- the sweat of his face. That type of change in living conditions is true death.

The Seven Dimensional Gospel

If you want to change a man who lives in the first dimension, you must persuade him of the benefits of something no lower than the second dimension. If you want to lift a man up from the second dimension, you must do so from no less than the third. If you want to reach a man in the third dimension, you must use a power that comes from no less than the fourth.

If you are preaching a second dimensional gospel, the highest converts you can have will be those of the second dimensional mind. If you are preaching a third dimensional gospel, you will not interest someone living in the fourth dimension. If you want to overcome the powers of the fourth, you must access the plan of the fifth.

The reason why we are not able to reach certain classes of people may be that they perceive our message as

> *If you are preaching a third dimensional gospel, you will not interest someone living in the fourth.*

being a gospel of a lower realm than where they are living at the time. You must demonstrate a power of a higher level if you want to get their attention. Many Americans have not turned to God although they have turned to the spirit world. Why?

The reason is because they have only associated the gospel of Jesus Christ with second or third dimensional living. Too many have relegated the gospel of Jesus Christ as something to be believed rather than a life to be lived. But God has designed for us to rise far above this. Jesus came that we might have life and have it more abundantly (John 10:10).

Too much of the so-called "Christian world" has settled for a social gospel or a moral gospel when they could have had so much better. Remember, just because you rise to a higher dimension does not mean you lose the "benefits" or "blessings" of the lower dimension. Just because you preach a greater, more powerful gospel does not mean you abandon the benefits (and obligations) of the social or moral gospel. It is simply that the greater encompasses and overwhelms the lesser.

Oh, that we may pray the prayer of the old hymn:

"My heart has no desire to stay
Where doubts arise and fears dismay;
Though some may dwell where these abound,
My prayer, my aim, is higher ground.

"I want to live above the world,
Though Satan's darts at me are hurled;
For faith has caught the joyful sound,
The song of saints on higher ground.

"I want to scale the utmost height,
And catch a gleam of glory bright;
But still I'll pray till Heaven I've found,
'Lord, lead me on to higher ground.'

"'Lord, lift me up and let me stand,
By faith on Heaven's tableland,
A higher plane than I have found;
Lord, plant my feet on higher ground.'"[6]

Paul said, "I press toward the goal for the prize of the upward call of God in Christ Jesus" (Philippians 3:14, NKJV). Let us press for the prize of the upward call of God. Let God lead you and plant your feet on higher ground. And proclaim the Gospel of Jesus Christ in the power and purity of the seventh dimension.

---

[6] Words by Johnson Oatman, Jr., music by Charles H. Gabriel, 1922.

"Lord, work in us to reconcile us to Your perfect will. Restore us to the great plan you have for us. Let the power of the Spirit of God work in us according to the will of God. Let us not be so easily influenced by our sinful natures. Help us to override the negative influences of fear, suspicion, hatred, criticism, doubt, selfishness, and every destructive force. Help us to flow with the faith of Your Spirit. Help us to be born again that we may enter into the Kingdom of God. Help us not to shortchange the gospel by suffocating it into the lower dimensional mindsets. Help us to preach it with all the glories of the seven dimensions of life. Plant our feet on higher ground. In Jesus' name."

PART II

CHAPTER EIGHT

● **LEARNING TO REIGN IN THE SPIRIT**

The Bible talks much about the kingdom of God, which is the domain of God's authority and power at work. In this kingdom, we are called to reign as kings and priests unto God (Revelation 1:6, 5:10). When some of the Pharisees asked Jesus when the kingdom of God would come, Jesus responded by saying that the kingdom of God would not come by observation (Luke 17:20).

Sometimes we act as if we must wait on God before we can see revival, growth, and the manifestation of the kingdom of God. We fall into a rut thinking that we can do nothing to see signs, wonders, and miracles. We are tempted to believe that we are powerless to work to see truth triumph, righteousness prevail, and godliness to be exalted. We may be conned into thinking that we cannot rise higher.[7] But the kingdom of God does not come with observation.

Jesus continued, "The kingdom of God is within you" (Luke 17:21). It is a spiritual kingdom. In part, this talks about ruling our own spirit, ruling who we are as individuals. Learning to reign in the kingdom of God starts with gaining dominion over yourself. The kingdom of God starts within you.

We talked about how the fifth dimension is one of perfect peace and dominion. To gain this dominion and peace, though, we must be in perfect alignment with the laws of life. Alignment in the spirit has to do with inward things, the matters of the heart. In this

---

[7]Of course, without God's help, we can rise no higher than the fourth dimension. No creature can rise any higher than one dimension from their normal state on their own (e.g., a dog can rise no higher than the third since his normal state is found in two dimensions).

part of the book, we will be exploring what it takes to have dominion, what it takes to reign as a king in the spirit. We will focus on getting ourselves in a position to be in alignment with God.

Learning to reign in the spirit starts with ruling over our own self, our own spirit. If we are to reign as kings and priests unto God in His kingdom, then we must start with ruling over ourselves. Before we can rule over the world and the angels, we must be able to rule over ourselves (I Corinthians 6:2-3). If we can be faithful over the little things, then God will make us ruler over the great things (Matthew 25:21, 23). To the extent that we rule faithfully over ourselves, we are able also to rule in the kingdom of God.

Paul wrote,

"Furthermore then we beseech you, brethren, and exhort *you* by the Lord Jesus, that as ye have received of us **how** ye ought **to walk and to please God**, *so* ye would abound more and more" (I Thessalonians 4:1).

The root of the Greek word behind "abound" is *perisuo* which means to increase, to be rendered more prominent, to be abundantly gifted, richly furnished, and to be possessed of a full sufficiency[8]. As we learn to walk with God and to please Him, we will be increased. We will become more spiritually prominent, which, I do not doubt, affects our prominence in this world.

This does not mean that we will always meet with this world's approval (I Corinthians 4:9-13). The world system will always chafe against the kingdom of God (Galatians 5:17). The flesh works contrary to the spirit. It is at a "right angle" with the spirit world.

But we are able to overcome this world (John 16:33). Our victory comes through our faith (I John 5:4). Our victories and our prominence are based in the spirit world (Acts 19:15). As we please God, we will also become more abundantly gifted in the spirit. But all this begins first with learning to please God.[9]

---

[8]"Perisuo," *The Analytical Greek Lexicon Revised*, ed. by Harold K. Moulton (Grand Rapids, Michigan: Zondervan Publishing House, 1978).

[9]This is not say that we earn any gift from God by merit. It is only to understand that God has put certain laws into place that govern the way He operates. He is a rewarder of those who will diligently seek Him (Hebrews 11:6). He rewards those who take the time to learn His ways.

Ruling over our Vessels

God desires that we should rule over our bodies, souls, and personalities. Paul went on to say,

"For this is the will of God, *even* your sanctification, that ye should abstain from fornication:
"That every one of you should **know how to possess** [TO GAIN MASTERY OVER OR TO RULE OVER] **his vessel in sanctification and honor**" (I Thessalonians 4:3-4).

Every one of us is to know how we are to gain the mastery over ourselves or to rule over our bodies and spirit. We are to learn to gain dominion over ourselves first. Then we pull down the strongholds of the enemy. This is done as we wrestle against the rulers of the darkness of this world and against spiritual wickedness in high places.

Spiritual warfare is done in the high places (the higher dimensions). Many are interested in spiritual warfare and destroying the works of the devil but they fail to understand that before we can successfully triumph over the enemy we must gain dominion over the self. In speaking about the high places, we will include the understanding of geographical locations. But more importantly, we will be referring to places in the higher dimensions. We will be speaking of high places within our lives, within our own hearts. These are the high places within our "vessels." Finally, we will be referring to strongholds in the spirit world.

I recognize that what I have written here may very easily be misunderstood. I may come down on some things very strongly. I am not saying that they are sin necessarily (as in that which commissions you to eternal damnation). I am simply trying to point out "high places." I am pointing out the way Satan's strongholds work.

I do not wish to be misunderstood so please read carefully. However, the best way to keep from being offended is to have an open and honest heart with God and a right spirit. We may encounter some touchy subjects but we are only trying to become willing to undergo the change necessary to rise into the higher dimensions.

Defining the High Places

The Book of Numbers tells an interesting story about how a certain king named Balak began to fear the Israelites. He decided that the only way to gain victory over them was to get a prophet of God to curse them. He found a willing accomplice in Balaam. It took some negotiating but Balak was finally able to enlist Balaam's services.

Numbers 22:41 records that Balak brought Balaam to the high places of Baal. When the time came for Balaam to find out what God wanted to do in the situation, he had Balak build seven altars. Together, they offered sacrifices to God.

Numbers 23:3 then refers to Balaam going to a high place to meet with God and to try to gain permission to curse His people. God was not

> *As a place of worship, a high place is where one interacts with the supernatural world.*

pleased with what Balaam had done. In His mercy, God began to work His own will in spite of Balaam and Balak's concerted attempts to thwart it. I refer to this scriptural passage because this incident records one of the first places in scripture to make reference to a high place.

In this case, this high place to which Balaam climbed was undoubtedly a height in elevation, a geographical location. But what is spoken of in the Old Testament as literal is often a reflection of the spiritual. The natural is often given to us as a picture of the spiritual. The physically high places around them were strongholds of Baal.

When the scriptures speak of a high place, it may be speaking of a height or high place in elevation geographically. At times, the connotation may be of a solitary place. In addition, the term is often used to refer to a place of strength.

In biblical times, most fortified cities and military fortifications were built on geographically high places. This was for strategic purposes. In their times, height was very valuable when it came time for battle.

If a city were in a valley, an opposing army could easily shoot their arrows of fire down into the city. They could more easily catapult their boulders over the walls that surrounded the city. They could more readily send men over the walls into the city in order to gain control over it.

On the other hand, if that city were built on a hill or mountain, it became much more difficult to shoot their arrows first up the hill and then over the walls. In addition, it made it more difficult for the opposing armies to send men over the walls. The people in the city could even use more primitive weapons to successfully resist the attack. As long as you were higher in elevation than the attacking armies, then you could rain down your own arrows or boulders on the enemy with much less effort. So cities and fortresses were often built on high places.

The high places were the locations where strongholds were built. Thus, the high places often became a place of great security. The word "high" was therefore used to refer to strength, power, and authority as well as elevation.

In most cases, as we shall see, the term "high place" refers to a place of worship. This reference is obviously to a physical place set aside for worship. But there is a spiritual dimension to this term as well. As a place of worship, it is a place where one can interact with the supernatural world. A physical place dedicated to worship is a place that has been set aside for the purpose of coming into contact with the supernatural world or the spiritual world.

When we worship God, we come into contact with God. He hears our prayers and answers them. He hears our worship or praise and receives it. When one worships an idol, they also come into contact with the spiritual world. Only now, they come in contact with evil spirits. Paul said, "The things which the Gentiles sacrifice, they sacrifice to devils" (I Corinthians 10:20). Whether the location is set aside for pagan worship or Christian worship, we understand high places are set aside for interaction with the spiritual world.

Paul said that when people sacrificed to idols, whether they knew it or not they were doing it to devils (I Corinthians 10:20). As long as they were involved in the act of sacrificing they were involved in worship. So it is that when we worship, we are coming into contact with the spiritual world. And a place set aside for worship or prayer is a place reserved for contact with the spiritual world.

Modern High Places

In every nation and kingdom, there are strongholds that help control that kingdom. There are military bases, economic bases, and political bases. These various strongholds are high places. In our modern day, locations that are known as being areas of great dignity or great advancement may be referred to as a high place. They are considered "high" because of their influence and because of their role as a center of commerce or a cultural center. Often, great economic powers reside there.

In our world, this would include places like New York City, Chicago, and Los Angeles. Any location that is a high place by one of these other definitions or

> **Locations which exercise great influence are spiritual strongholds.**

standards is also a high place spiritually. If we desire to turn our nation, state, or region to the Lord we will have to gain dominion over the high places that rule these areas.

Because of the great influence of universities, any town that is home to a large or influential university also can be viewed as a high place. Thus, even though Cambridge, Massachusetts, is not a large city, it is a spiritual high place because of Harvard University. New Haven, Connecticut, is a high place because of Yale University. Likewise, Charlottesville, Virginia, is a high place because of the University of Virginia. Great power and influence emanates from these places.

A city that is the capital of a nation or from which a king reigns could be referred to as a high place. Washington, D.C. is, without a doubt, a high place. The same goes for London, England, and Moscow, Russia. It would also include any city that is a political seat of power, such as the capitol city of a state or a county seat. They are considered "high" because of their political power.

With regards to false gods or to worship of a false god, the cities that are homes to great followings that are not based on scripture may also be seen as high places (strongholds) of the enemy. This would include all "exalted places" or any place that is considered of great honor to a particular religion. Examples of these types of high places would be Mecca (a holy city to the Muslims), Rome (home of Roman Catholicism), and Salt Lake City (home of Mormonism). In addition, any place that is the home to a "sacred temple" may also be considered a high place.

Places that are known for being centers of crime are high places spiritually. Cities that are centers of wickedness are high places. Examples may be San Francisco, Las Vegas, and New Orleans. Satanic forces sup their venom from these high places. We wrestle against spiritual wickedness in high places.

The Command to Eliminate the High Places

Initially, when Israel worshipped Yahweh (their name for the LORD) in the high places God tolerated it. Of course, it was only tolerated as long as they would only worship Him in those high places. If they worshipped other gods, it obviously became unacceptable.

I Samuel 9 records the story of Saul first meeting the prophet Samuel. According to verses 12-14, when Saul came to the city where Samuel was, he was told that he could find the man of God on the way going up to a high place. The people were going to sacrifice there. So we could surmise that at least at one point, it was fairly common practice as well as being tolerated by God.

In I Chronicles 21:28-30, when David built his altar in Ornan's threshing floor, it was not in opposition to the temple (since it had not yet been built) but in concurrence with it. He did it in obedience to the angel of the Lord and because of the present distress. He was in an urgent situation with lives at stake. In this case, it was not a matter of convenience as much as a matter of obedience to the angel of the Lord. Also keep in mind that the temple was not yet built.

So God initially tolerated true worship being done in the high places. But once they entered into the promised land, they were to follow God's command that they were to destroy all the high places of the pagans (Numbers 33:52). He left no room for exceptions. He told them to "...destroy all their pictures, and destroy all their molten images, and quite pluck down all their high places."

In Deuteronomy 12:1-14, Moses reminded them that once they entered the promised land, they were to destroy all the high places and only to worship God in the one place where He decided to place His name. Once the temple site was chosen, it would no longer be acceptable to sacrifice in the exalted (high) places.

In time, God chose Jerusalem as the city where His name would dwell and the place where His Spirit would shine. In our day, God has decided to put His name on a people and His Presence (Spirit) in their hearts. That is now our solitary place (our altar). We do not have to travel to a certain city to offer sacrifice to God and to see the Shekinah glory of God. We can offer sacrifice from the altar of our hearts. We are the temple of the Holy Ghost (I Corinthians 3:16). His glory is to shine from our lives and our spirit.

In Old Testament times, the one place of worship (or the one place of sacrifice) also signified unity. The nation was to be unified in their place of worship. Their focus was to be centralized.

In our day, our worship to God must also be unified. We cannot serve two masters (Matthew 6:24). We must choose one and give Him all or we will be serving the other by default. It has been said that either Jesus is Lord over all in our lives or else He is not Lord at all.

We can only serve one master when it comes to our walk with God. We cannot have split

> **The one place of worship signified unity of spirit.**

loyalties. Many think that they are serving God while the reality is that their job is their biggest pursuit. For others it may be pleasure. It is not possible for pleasure to be your greatest pursuit and for your master to be the Lord Jesus at the same time. If your chief interest is money, your master cannot be the Lord.

Jesus said, "Blessed are the pure in heart, for they shall see God" (Matthew 5:8). Our hearts must be pure if we intend to see the glory of God. The term "pure gold" is used to refer to a substance that has nothing else in it other than gold. It has no other chemicals. It is singularly gold. So also if we intend to see the glory of God, our hearts must be pure.

"One moment we make decisions on the basis of sound reason and the next moment out of fear of what others will think of us."[10] This statement made by Richard Foster reveals what purity of heart is not. Soren Kierkegaard wrote a book with a profound title: Purity of Heart is to Will One Thing. Purity of heart is having a single desire. Purity of heart is not being double minded.

We must have a single focus. We dare not be double minded for James said, "let not that man think that he shall receive any thing of the Lord. A double minded man *is* unstable in all his ways" (James 1:7-8). Our eye must be single. I do not want to be among those who cannot expect to receive anything from God. I want God to hear my prayers.

---

[10] Richard J. Foster, *Celebration of Discipline* (New York, NY: HarperCollins Publishers, 1978), Revised Edition, 80.

Spiritual Harlotry

Is it possible to serve the one true God and another god as well? Is it conceivable that we allow high places to remain in our lives while thinking we are serving God alone? Is it possible to live for God without tearing down all of Satan's strongholds in our lives? Can we love God without loving Him with all of our heart, soul, mind, and strength?

I will answer these questions with a question. Is it possible for a harlot to have more than one lover? This is precisely how Israel is described in Scripture. In fact, one prophet's whole ministry consisted in showing Israel that they were playing the harlot in their worship of the Lord. That prophet was Hosea. He was even told to go out and marry a harlot just to prove the point.

We play the harlot with God when we think that it is okay to follow after this world. This hurts our relationship with the Husband of the Church.

"You ask and do not receive, because you ask amiss, that you may spend *it* on your pleasures.

"Adulterers and adulteresses! Do you not know that friendship with the world is enmity with God? Whoever therefore wants to be a friend of the world makes himself an enemy of God" (James 4:3-4, NKJV).

Again, I want to be among those who receive answers to their prayers. When I ask, I want to receive. We cannot do things with the stamp of approval from a carnal mindset and still be right with God. "Set your affection on things above, not on things on the earth" (Colossians 3:2). We are to seek out life in the higher dimensions.

If we are looking to two different worlds we will not think right. If we try to serve two masters we will find that we have capitulated to darkness. If we eat of the tree of knowledge of good and evil, we will find that evil begins to rule our lives. A little leaven will leaven the whole lump. One of Satan's most successful lies is that "a little bit won't hurt." If we have a pure heart, a single focus in our pursuit of God, the whole body will be full of His light (Matthew 6:22). But this requires our eye (desire) to be single.

Scripture refers to some who lived for God with a perfect heart. This does not mean perfect in the sense of being without a flaw. We understand that this is not possible as far as human beings are concerned, especially considering our sinful nature. We all have our weaknesses.

Walking before God with a perfect heart refers to serving God with our whole heart. Our hearts must be unified in our search for God or our pursuit of Him. Only then can we find Him. "Ye shall seek me, and find me, when ye shall search for me with all your heart" (Jeremiah 29:13). We must not have a divided allegiance. We can only serve one master.

As God tried to teach the Israelites, we must only worship the one true God. Our worship must be directed to Him alone. We cannot split our worship between the Lord and some other god. And we must have one place of worship (I am not talking about a physical place but I will speak more on that later).

Looking the Other Way

After the temple was built, the Israelites neglected to obey God's command to destroy all the high places. As long as these high places were around, people continued to offer sacrifices there. It was a temptation that was too easy to resist.

In fact, rather than destroying them, they often continued to erect them. When the high places were built after the construction of the temple, at the very least they were built in competition with the temple, which was the one chosen place of worship. Sometimes they were made in direct opposition to the temple as a result of rebellion.

Obviously, it was more convenient to offer a sacrifice in a high place than it was to travel to Jerusalem to do so. The high

> *Tearing down the high places will not be as easy as allowing them to exist.*

places were so much closer. Going to Jerusalem was so much work and trouble. In our lives, tearing down the high places will not be as easy as allowing them to exist. Tearing down the high places and going only "to Jerusalem" will seem such an inconvenience. But do not let convenience dictate your walk with God. If you are going to be a disciple, you must be willing to deny yourself and take up your cross. Do not worry. The reward of dominion will be worth it.

When Solomon and the congregation went to sacrifice in Gibeah in I Kings 3 (where God appeared to him and gave him wisdom), he went because the tabernacle of the Lord was there (II Chronicles 1:3-5). It was expected that he go where the tabernacle of the Lord was.

> **Do not allow convenience to dictate your walk with God.**

Up until the time the temple was built, the Israelites were expected to go to wherever the tabernacle of the Lord was. When there was no distress pressing them, as there had been in David's aforementioned example, they were expected to travel to the place of the tabernacle.

Solomon, though, did not always do this.

"Only the people sacrificed in high places, because there was no house built unto the name of the LORD, until those days.

And Solomon loved the LORD, walking in the statutes of David his father: only he sacrificed and burnt incense in high places" (I Kings 3:2-3).

Some things God allows. However, just because He allows it does not mean that He is pleased with it. The mention of Solomon going to the other high places is recorded here as a statement of disappointment. But when he went to the place of the tabernacle to sacrifice, God rewarded him greatly.

As a result of Solomon seeking the Lord on His terms, he was granted wisdom from God and turned into a builder. Wisdom turns people into builders of one sort or another. Wisdom builds rather than destroys.

> **Big surrenders result from many little surrenders.**

It is wise men that build nations, organizations, churches, families, and people. They build these things up rather than tear them down. Foolish people tear things down. Any fool can cause a nation to self-destruct and decay in immorality. Any fool can run an organization into the ground. Any fool can steer a corporation into bankruptcy. It takes wisdom to grow a company, to gain market share, to succeed.

Foolish men and women split churches through rebellion. Fools destroy families and people. Foolish people destroy their brothers and sisters with their tongues. But wise men and women will build or edify them. "Through wisdom is an house builded" (Proverbs 24:1-4).

When God gives us a gift, we can use it for good or for evil. At first, Solomon used his wisdom to build the temple in Jerusalem and his palace. Then he began to build great cities and storehouses in Israel.

But in his old age his ungodly wives turned his heart away from serving only the one true God. "His heart was not perfect with the LORD his God" according to I Kings 11:4. Verses 5-8 show how he began to worship other gods and eventually used his gift in building things to make that which displeased the Lord.

He began to build high places (places of worship) to other gods. These were strongholds for the pagan gods. How was Solomon able to make such a big surrender to the enemy considering his earlier walk with God? Big surrenders result from many little surrenders. We, too, sometimes take a gift that God has given us and use it to do things that displease Him.

Some will take their gift of a good singing voice or some other musical ability and use it not to edify and

> *More dangerous than the enemy without is the enemy within.*

build up the people of God but rather to encourage that which is wrong. Others take the gifts God has given them in administration or organization and use it simply for this world's wealth or maybe even to build a system of criminal activity. So they use their gift for organized crime rather than to work good. Still others will take the good looks or attractive bodies they were blessed with and use them in prostitution or some act of pornography. Yet others will take the natural strength they have and use it for violence.

We can use our talents and skills for various means that may even be "good" but if we exalt those things higher than our service to God, we build high places in our lives. These high places will prove to be our downfall as they proved to work towards the downfall of Solomon spiritually.

Eventually, the Lord determined to take the greater measure of the kingdom away from him. If we insist on building high places in our lives that displease God, is it unthinkable that He would be moved to take at least a measure of the kingdom away from us? He did say, "I *am* the Lord, I change not" (Malachi 3:6). Which kingdom is it that we are involved in? It is the kingdom of God of which Jesus spoke. Faithfulness over the little things such as the high places will make us ruler over great things (Matthew 25:21, 23).

Approved High Places

In honor of Solomon's father (David), God waited until Solomon died before He tore the bigger part of the kingdom away from him. Jeroboam then led the northern ten tribes in revolt against Solomon's son, Rehoboam.

When Jeroboam gained the bigger part of the kingdom, he feared the return of his followers to the house of David. So he built two calves for the northern tribes to worship. This way they would not have to go to Jerusalem to sacrifice. Notice that he did not necessarily introduce other gods to them. He did not send them to other gods. He simply told them that these calves were the gods that delivered Israel out of Egypt (I Kings 12:28-31). This was a perversion of the one true God. Surely they had been delivered from Egypt but it was not the result of some golden calves made by man.

I suppose it could be said that Jeroboam tried to worship the one true God with false images. But even if this was so, he violated the ten commandments by using the false images.

"Thou shalt have no other gods before me.

"Thou shalt not make unto thee any graven image, or any likeness *of any thing* that *is* in heaven above, or that *is* in the earth beneath, or that *is* in the water under the earth:

"Thou shalt not bow down thyself to them, nor serve them: for I the LORD thy God *am* a jealous God" (Exodus 20:3-5b).

As if that were not enough wrong done, Jeroboam went beyond the making of the golden calves to making a "house of high places" or an organization of high places. He established a system or worship based on using the high places.

> **When you allow the enemy to build strongholds within your gates, you set yourself up for a fall.**

For this cause God sent a prophet to him with a message of judgment. According to I Kings 13:6-7 and 33-34, Jeroboam was moved but did not change. Too often we allow ourselves to be moved without determining to change. Scripture states that "this thing became sin" to his house. Why? Because they went from bad to worse. They descended into downright idolatry.

With these high places, they established strongholds for the enemy in their own land. More dangerous than the enemy without is the enemy within. And when you allow the enemy to build strongholds within your gates, you set yourself up for a fall.

The people of Israel may have started worshipping God in the high places but they soon slid to outright paganism. They quickly went to worshipping false gods in those high places. Eventually, God brought those northern ten tribes into captivity because of their sins.

Jeroboam's sin was the beginning of the end for the northern tribes of Israel. Because of their pride and unwillingness to submit themselves back to David's authority, they never did repent. This caused them to invent another way to worship God. But God was not pleased with it.

"Lord, help us not to allow convenience or our flesh to dictate our walk with you. Let us not be guilty of spiritual harlotry. Strengthen us to stop the enemy from building strongholds in our lives. Help us to be unified in our spirit and will when we come to you. Help us to rule over our vessels with honor and in sanctification. In Jesus' name."

CHAPTER NINE

FLIRTING WITH HIGH PLACES
Rehoboam's Weakness

Let us briefly follow the history of the nation of Judah to see how the high places affected them. According to II Chronicles 11:13-17, certain people left Jeroboam and his ways. They went down from the north to Jerusalem to sacrifice to the Lord. These were the priests and the Levites along with all those who had "set their hearts to seek the LORD". Those who had set their hearts to please God refused to enter into a corrupted worship of God. They left their homes and their possessions because a pure worship of God was more important to them.

Even today, when people who have set their hearts to seek the Lord realize that they are in a high place, they will leave their high places. They will search out those who seek the Lord with a pure heart.

Unfortunately, Rehoboam (king over Judah) did not prepare his heart to seek the Lord according to II Chronicles 12:13-14. This caused Judah to work evil under Rehoboam. He did not consciously set his mind to seek after God so those who followed him fell into sin. The natural end result of not making such a conscious decision to seek God is doing evil.

How did they do evil? I Kings 14:21-24 explains how it started. They built high places throughout the land and thus provoked the Lord to jealousy. They must have thought that if Solomon and Jeroboam could get away with it (seemingly) that they should be able to get away with it as well.

Verse 21 makes specific reference to the one place where God decided to put His name among the people of Israel, which was Jerusalem. Verse 22 says they did evil and provoked the Lord to jealousy. Verse 23 explains that they did this by building the high places. As a result, verse 24 tells us that sodomites (homosexuals) began to rise throughout the nation.

Both of the books of the Bible that record Rehoboam's history (I Kings and II Chronicles) mention his mother, an Ammonitess. She was able to influence Judah to sin because Rehoboam was weak. He was weak because he did not set his heart to seek the Lord.

You cannot be strong until you know God (Dan 6:32). You cannot know God (or anyone, for that matter) until

> **Your worship cannot be pure if your lifestyle is corrupt.**

you find Him and "meet" Him. You cannot find Him until you seek Him diligently (Hebrews 11:6) with all your heart (Jeremiah 29:13).

Rehoboam's mother was not a Jew but an Ammonitess. She was not a descendant of Abraham but of Lot. As a result of his travels with Abraham, Lot did believe in the worship of the one true God. But living in Sodom tended to have its corrupting influence on Lot's children, if not Lot himself.

Lot finally managed to get a couple of daughters out of Sodom (with the help of a couple of angels) but he failed to get Sodom out of them. Their lifestyles became corrupted. And their worship of God became corrupted for your worship cannot be pure if your lifestyle is corrupt.

As a descendant of Lot, Rehoboam's mother believed in worship to the one true God but, having been corrupted by Sodom as Lot's kids were, she also served other gods. This pattern of thinking took hold of Rehoboam and the kingdom of Judah. They built high places for worship of other gods (following Solomon's example). The influence of Sodom over Rehoboam's mother is the reason for the rise of homosexuality in Judah during the reign of Rehoboam (I Kings 14:24).

The first commandment God gave to Moses was, "Thou shalt have no other gods before me" (Exodus 20:3). God wants all of you, not just a part of you. Some of the other nations of the Old Testament did serve the Yahweh God of Israel in part. They did this at times because they knew of His prophets and Israel's glorious kings. They had heard of God's mighty acts so they would serve Him to a degree.

But they did not serve Him exclusively. God has always wanted a people that would serve Him exclusively, without reservations. God wanted Israel to be an example to the whole world of serving Him only. They failed miserably.

After Rehoboam died, Abijam ruled Judah for three years. I Kings 15:3 says that "he walked in all the sins of his father." So Judah continued doing corruptly. The high places continued to flourish.

Asa's Influence

Next, Asa came to the throne of Judah. His name means "physician" or "cure." He helped to heal the hurt of his people by destroying the worship of false gods in the high places. He also took away the high places out of the **cities** of Judah (II Chronicles 14:2-5). Paganism was removed. This is noted as being pleasing to God for it was good and right in His eyes. Therefore, they had peace from their enemies for ten years (II Chronicles 14:1, 6).

> *God desires that we use all of our influence to promote good.*

According to I Kings 15:11-14, Asa put out the sodomites (homosexuals) from their land and removed the idols. He even destroyed his own mother's idol and removed her from being queen. But a statement of regret is issued in the Word of God in that the high places were not destroyed altogether. He destroyed the high places from being in the cities of Judah but perhaps did not destroy them out of the countryside altogether.

In II Chronicles 15:17, a statement of disappointment again is issued in that the high places were not removed in Israel. According to II Chronicles 15:9, we understand that Asa had influence in Israel (the northern ten tribes). But he did not use that influence to cause them to remove their high places. God desires that we use all of our influence to promote good.

> *High places work to undermine our faith.*

Towards the end of his reign, Asa's faith in God grew weak. Earlier in his life he had depended on God to grant him victory against an army of one million Ethiopians. But later, against Baasha, king of Israel, he depended on the Syrians for help instead of seeking the hand of God. When we allow high places to remain, we will find that they work to undermine our faith.

Also, in the matter of his diseased feet he did not seek to the Lord but to the physicians (II Chronicles 16:12). Therefore, he never did gain complete healing concerning his foot problems.

Indeed, his feet became worse. He died two years later. As a result of this weakness of faith, some of the high places probably began to regain prominence in the cities of Judah. More importantly, the worship of false gods in the high places began to reenter the mainstream.

We must ever stay vigilant concerning our faith and the exercise of our faith or we will allow high places (Satan's strongholds) to begin creeping back into our lives. In turn, those high places will work to undermine our faith in God. Just as the earth continually produces thorns and thistles since man's fall, so our hearts continually produce evil desires (Mark 7:20-23). Jude exhorted us to earnestly contend for the faith which was once delivered to the saints (Jude 3).

The next king of Judah was Jehoshaphat. He followed after God and even renewed some of the cleansing that his father Asa had started,

> *We must ever guard the exercise of our faith or we will allow Satan's strongholds to creep into our lives.*

such as removing the remnant of the sodomites. In the early years of his reign he began to remove the high places out of Judah (II Chronicles 17:6). He also destroyed the pagan worship (the groves) that had crept back into the kingdom as a result of his father's lack of faith.

Because Jehoshaphat did this, God blessed him greatly. In fact, all the gentile kingdoms around Judah had the fear of God in them because of Jehoshaphat's zeal for God (II Chronicles 17:10). It is amazing how people around you will develop a fear of God when you manifest a great zeal for God.

Unfortunately, after a number of years, Jehoshaphat's zealousness began to wane and he began to have some evil associations such as his friendship with

> *It is amazing how people around you will develop a fear of God when you manifest a great zeal for God.*

Ahab, Jezebel's husband. When we quit contending for the faith, we tend to develop friendships with those who lead us away from the true faith.

We must guard against letting our zealousness for God to wane over time. Some start out on fire for God but after a while, they become "familiar" with the things of God so that it no longer has a hold of them as in their younger years. This does not come from wisdom or maturity. This comes from laziness of spirit. Oh, that we may always continue our pursuit of God.

As a result of these evil affiliations which Jehoshaphat developed, some of the high places began to sprout up again so that at the end of his reign, a mark is written against him in scripture. I Kings 22:43 and II Chronicles 20:33 issue God's common complaint against some of His people in that the high places were not taken away.

The Bible does not specify that they worshipped false gods in these high places as of yet. Regardless, the simple fact that they had them did not please God. It can be argued that they did not serve Baal or Ashtoreth or some other false god. They may have only worshipped the one true God. Nevertheless, God's disappointment is still noted. "The people offered and burnt incense yet in the high places."

> *When we stop contending for the faith, we tend to develop friendships with those who lead us away from the faith.*

Jehoram was Judah's next king. Having married Ahab's daughter, he was heavily influenced by their wicked ways. Therefore, he was an evil king. Obviously, not only the high places flourished but also the worship of pagan gods and all the correlated sins (II Chronicles 21:10-11). We should be careful whom we choose to marry since it will greatly influence our future.

Ahaziah was next to come to the throne. He also was an evil king, walking in the ways of the wicked kings of Israel. So under him paganism continued to grow and with it the number of high places. He was killed with the king of Israel when Jehu broke Ahab's power in the northern tribes.

> *Wickedness spreads much more quickly when wicked people are in power.*

Then Athaliah, his mother, ruled over Judah after killing all of the royal seed (or so she thought, for one of the king's seed was rescued and raised in the temple). She was very wicked. Therefore, wickedness prevailed even more so in the land of Judah. Wickedness will always spread much more quickly when wicked people are in leadership. In our day, we have a responsibility to do our part to help righteous men rule and keep wicked men out of power.

Jehoash's Hardened Heart

Jehoash (Joash) reigned over Judah next, being the one who was rescued from Athaliah's murderous acts. Jehoash was raised in the temple by Jehoida the priest. As long as Jehoiada the priest was alive and guided him, Jehoash did well. Some people can live for God as long as a particular person or situation is present. But when that person is removed (whether by death, job transfer, or otherwise) or when the situation has changed, they begin to slip away.

Yet, even while Jehoiada the priest was alive, Jehoash did not do as well as he could have. The statement of disappointment is issued in that the high places were not

> *We can remove all the sins from our lives without necessarily removing all the strongholds or the high places.*

taken away (II Kings 12:2-3). Again, the people may not necessarily have engaged in heathen worship in the high places. They may have worshipped only the one true God but it was not what God desired. The high places were not destroyed like they should have been. Therefore, the statement of regret is written.

Afterwards, when Jehoiada the priest was dead, the people of Judah resorted to heathen worship (II Chronicles 24:17-18). Since the high places were already being used, it made it convenient to begin worship of the false gods.

We can remove all the sins in our lives without necessarily removing all the strongholds or the high places. If we stop committing adultery, that is good. But if we continue to spend time entertaining those thoughts, the strongholds will remain in our hearts. If we continue to view pornographic material, the high places remain in our lives and we set ourselves up for a fall. The strongholds of lust remain to interfere with our reign in the spirit.

If we quit burglarizing homes -- wonderful! But if we glory in our past sinful lives, the high places have not been removed. Our thinking still favors those sins. Our heart is still there, worshipping in those high places.

In the early part of Jehoash's reign, the high places remained, even though the idols and the pagan worship were removed. Though the people

> *God notices the details of our hearts.*

made good sacrifices on the high places, yet they lost respect (or in some cases, never gained respect) for the **details** of God's Word.

They disregarded the details where God specified that He wanted them to sacrifice only in the temple, where He had placed His name.

Many have lost respect for the sacredness of the one high place where the tabernacle of the Lord dwells. Many have lost respect for the one way of worship that pleases God (that is, worshipping Him in spirit and in truth). The details of certain commandments of God's Word are looked at as being insignificant. They believe that you can just explain away certain scriptures that you don't like and everything will be okay. Being sacrilegious is no longer viewed as being offensive.

Details can indeed be very important. Even after Moses had seen the burning bush and received the call of God on his life to go to Egypt to demand that Pharaoh let them go, Moses did not have everything in order according to the details of God's commandments. Moses had received the signs from God about his calling. The rod had been turned into a snake and back into the rod again. He had heard the audible voice of God.

Moses had submitted to authority in gaining permission from his father-in-law to leave. God even spoke to him again while he was in Midian to encourage him to go to Egypt and to inform him that all of his enemies were dead. But while Moses went to do the will of God, the LORD met him in the way to kill him. What saved his life was Zipporah (his wife) circumcising their son (Exodus 3:1-4:26). It seemed like a small, insignificant detail compared with the great call of God. But it almost cost him his life.

The lack of this simple detail (circumcision of their children) may have undermined the faith of the people of Israel to enter into the promised land. The people that came out of Egypt did not circumcise their sons as the Lord commanded them (Joshua 5:5-7). The Lord had commanded Joshua to do it before they could possess the land. The reproach of Egypt could not be wiped away until it was done. Details are important.

It was a small detail that caused Joshua's men to lose the battle against Ai. It was a small thing Achan did in taking a few of the spoils of war for himself. But God regards details. Details are important.

Some have seen a tremendous loss of the fear of God. They are not worried about the consequences of their actions and words. They are not concerned about the wages of sin. What they care about is looking good to people rather than being right with the Lord.

These people often become legalistic in one form or another -- and not all legalism is on the conservative end. Sometimes they are looking for loopholes that seem to allow them to indulge in their sin. That is also legalism -- splitting hairs on the commands of God.

Some revel in their idea of "living in their liberties." I am all in favor of being given the freedom to walk in the liberties that we may have. But this gives us no excuse to indulge the lusts of our flesh. Paul said, "*use* not liberty for an occasion to the flesh" (Galatians 5:13).

All these situations indicate the existence of high places among us. When we do not get rid of the high places in our lives, it displeases God and we set

> **When we have hardened our hearts to God's messengers, we will stop at nothing to escape hearing the call to repentence.**

ourselves up for a fall. Some things may not be "heaven or hell" issues but that does not mean that we should indulge in it. "All things are lawful for me, but all things are not helpful. All things are lawful for me, but I will not be brought under the power of any" (I Corinthians 6:12, NKJV). Paul says it again four chapters later, "All things are lawful for me, but not all things are helpful; all things are lawful for me, but not all things edify" (I Corinthians 10:23, NKJV). Surely God is a God of great mercy. But He is also a jealous God.

When God tried to warn Jehoash through the prophet Zechariah, their hearts were so hardened that they conspired to stone him to death (II Chronicles 24:20-22). Zechariah was the son of Jehoiada the priest. Jehoash could not even show kindness to the son of the man who had been so kind to him. He probably excused himself by saying that Zechariah was being too "puritan" or moralistic.

Often, when we have hardened our hearts to God's messengers, we will stop at nothing to escape hearing the call to repentance. The last part of Jehoash's life was spent being spoiled by the Syrians and living in great diseases (perhaps an infected wound). Sin has a way of stripping us of blessings that God has given to us which only He can give.

Imperfect Hearts

Amaziah was the next king over Judah. He was a good king generally but not with a perfect heart (II Kings 14:3-4, II Chronicles

25:2). He was like those who are "good people" and serve God but they do not have a perfect heart toward God. Their heart is not fully set towards God. They are not "sold out." They are just good people but do not ask them to do any task for God that would inconvenience them. At least, do not ask them to do it for long or do not ask them to make a major commitment. They do not have a passionate love for God, the things of God, and the people of God.

Amaziah served God like his father Jehoash did. He was "good" but not with a perfect heart. He allowed the high places to remain. Amaziah eventually lost respect for the man of God. A natural consequence of the existence of high places is that we will lose proper respect for the man of God. We disdain spiritual authority. We begin to view people of prayer with contempt. Amaziah eventually also bowed before the gods of the heathen. Once the high places are in place and flourishing in our lives, it is usually not too long before we find ourselves bowing in slavery to the enemy.

> *A natural consequence of the existence of high places is that we will lose proper respect for the man of God.*

Azariah (Uzziah) was Judah's next ruler. He also was like his father (II Kings 15:3-4, II Chronicles 26:4-5). He worshipped the one true God. But again, the now famous statement of regret is issued concerning this king. The high places were not removed. The worship of false gods was removed initially and the worship of the LORD (Yahweh) was instituted. But the high places themselves were not removed.

Scripture tells us that as long as the prophet Zechariah was around, Azariah did well and sought after God. But when that influence was removed, Azariah lost out with God because he did not serve God with a perfect heart. The natural is often a picture of the spiritual. The high places of his heart were not removed just as the high places in his kingdom were not removed.

He eventually also lost respect for the man of God. He thought he could do everything on his own and did not need the man of God. He went into the temple to burn incense on the altar of incense. The priests of the Lord tried to warn him against doing this. But instead of listening to them, he became angry with them. He became furious that the man of God would stop him from doing wrong, from doing his own thing.

God then judged him with the curse of leprosy (II Chronicles 26:16-21). Azariah was a leper until his death. We should be careful lest we get judged for hardening our heart against someone who tries to warn us from doing wrong or "doing our own thing."

Some people will only live for God as Jehoash or Azariah did. They will serve Him but not with a perfect heart (not with **all** or **the completeness of** their heart). They are trying to serve two masters at the same time. They are trying to live in two different kingdoms (God's and Satan's) at the same time. They are being double minded.

They may manage to do well for a while. But when the man of God in their life is removed, they fall by the wayside. If they should move to another city where they are no longer in close contact with their pastor or the person who birthed them into the kingdom of God, they lose out with God. If God should call their pastor to go to another place, they become unfaithful and eventually wither up and die spiritually.

Jotham was next on the throne of Judah. He served God in the same way as his father did except that he took time to prepare his ways before the Lord (II Kings 15:34-35, II Chronicles 27:2,6). Therefore, he did do a little better than his fathers. Yet, like many that had gone on before, he failed to take away the high places. Therefore, "the people did yet corruptly."

It was good that Jotham did well. But he did not influence those under his leadership to do well. We do well when we live for God even when no one is following us in doing so. We do better when we influence them to do the same. Some people seem to think that because others who have served God in the past did not take down certain high places, that they are also excused from doing so. But as was noted in Jotham's case, it still was not pleasing to God.

Ahaz was Judah's next ruler. He was a wicked king (II Chronicles 28:2-4,25). Not only did he not take the high places away, he openly engaged in heathen worship. He went so far as to participate in the satanic ritual of burning his children in the fire. As a result of all this, the judgment of God fell on Judah. "The LORD brought Judah low because of Ahaz king of Israel; for he made Judah naked, and transgressed sore against the LORD" (II Chronicles 28:19).

During Ahaz's reign over Judah, the nation of Israel (the northern 10 tribes) was taken into captivity. This is why Ahaz is referred to as being the king of Israel. He was king over what was left of the original nation of Israel. But he learned no lesson from the captivity of the northern tribes.

Divided Loyalties

It is interesting to note the reasons scripture gives us for the captivity of the northern ten tribes as found in II Kings 17:9-23. At first, the children of Israel "did secretly *those* things that *were* not right against the LORD their God" (verse 9). Where did these secret sins start? Verses 9-12 explain that this happened in the high places. Likewise, the secret sins of the "kingdoms" of our heart will begin in the high places that we do not tear down.

Verse 15 tells us that they followed vanity. Vanity would be that which is void of profit spiritually. In a truly Christian atmosphere, we do not seek after vanity. Only in a "Christian" world where high places abound would vanity be much sought after and followed.

> *The end result of one who refuses to destroy the high places in his life is the condition of being held captive by the enemy.*

Today, many will pay big money to see a "Christian" comedian or entertainment when they will not give in the offering to help a true man of God to preach the gospel or to a missionary to carry out his burden. They love going to concerts but going to the prayer room is too much work. Staying up all night sounds great unless it means an all night prayer meeting. To keep up with the sports page is a welcome idea but to study the scriptures is considered burdensome. Spiritual things are not welcomed into their life. If they are accepted, it is done grudgingly. These attitudes show that they are following after vanity. They are pursuing things that do not bring any substantive benefit.

You may ask, "What is the harm of following vanity?" What was the result of their following vanity? Verse 15 states that they became vain and became like the heathen around them. Many today who have refused to destroy their high places have become vain themselves. They have decided that it is not such a bad thing to be like the world though God has commanded His people that we ought to come out from the world and be separate.

Verses 16 and 17 show how they began to worship other gods and eventually engaged in occult activities. As a result, "the LORD rejected all the seed of Israel" (Verse 20). They were led away as captives. The end result of one who refuses to destroy the high places in his life is the condition of being held captive by the enemy.

The final condition of one who wants to go to the higher dimensions without a pure heart is the captivity of the lower dimensions. The deceiver will try to get people to think that they can do so without a pure heart. They may believe they can access the powers of the higher dimensions for the benefits of a lower nature. But it does not work that way.

"Be not deceived; God is not mocked: for whatsoever a man soweth, that shall he also reap.

"For he that soweth to his flesh [THE DESIRES OF THE LOWER NATURE] shall of the flesh reap corruption; but he that soweth to the Spirit, shall of the Spirit reap life everlasting"(Galatians 6:7-8).

If we sow to the desires of the lower nature and allow the high places to remain in our lives, we will reap the destruction of the lower dimensions. But if we sow to the desires of the Spirit of God, we reap the life of the higher dimensions.

President Eisenhower once made the statement, "There are no victories at bargain prices." You can either pay the price for true victory now or wait till later to pay the price. But if you wait till later you will find the price has gone up because of "inflation" -- you will have to pay interest. There are no easy shortcuts to sainthood. There are no discounts on the price of true spiritual victory.

Verses 24-26 describe the how the king of Assyria brought numbers of the heathen to dwell in the land vacated by Israel. At first, these Gentiles did not fear the Lord. They did their own thing. They worked their own will. But when God sent lions among them to destroy them, they decided that they needed to learn "the manner of the God of the land." They wanted relief from the lions.

So they brought one of the priests who had been carried away into captivity to teach them the manner of the God of the land. He taught them how to fear the Lord. But it seems that the priests still had not learned their lesson concerning high places and worship of the Lord alone. Or at the very least, the Assyrians did not learn it well. They refused to get rid of their other gods.

In addition, they allowed folks to become priests who were the worst among them. These priests were the ones who sacrificed in the high places. It really does pay to set a high standard for the ministry. We do not want to be guilty of allowing the lowest or the basest of people to enter the ministry.

"They feared the LORD, and served their own gods" (II Kings 17:33). Many today fear the Lord but they serve their own gods. They wear the "Christian" nametag but they live according to their own pleasures. They do not take into account how the Lord is a jealous God. They have a respect and reverence for God but they live according to the desires of their flesh.

Verse 41 sums up the disgust God had with these Gentiles that took over the land and lived in this manner. "So these nations feared the LORD, and served their graven images." The LORD did not judge these Gentiles because they were new to the ways of God, unlike the people of Israel. They did not "know better." They were still in the time period when God winked at their ignorance. But now God commands "all men everywhere to repent" (Acts 17:30).

The Influence of High Places

In continuing our journey through the history of the nation of Judah, we find that Hezekiah was their next king. He must have learned some lessons from how the LORD judged the northern tribes of Israel. Scripture tells us that he not only did right in the sight of the Lord but that he did it according to his father David (II Kings 18:3-7). What did he do to merit being mentioned as serving God like David did? He removed the high places in the land in addition to destroying heathen worship.

Unfortunately, Manasseh was the next king over Judah. He was a very wicked king initially. He not only built up the high places which his father had destroyed but he openly engaged in the worship of other gods. In addition, he freely indulged into witchcraft (II Kings 21:1-7). He even flaunted his wickedness in the face of God by building altars to other gods in the house of the Lord.

Shocking as it may seem, the "Christian world" has many of these types of people. Too many build altars to other gods or powers in the house of the Lord. Some have Christian gatherings but instead of exalting Jesus Christ and the ways of God, they are only interested in partying (reveling) and having a good time. They only want to satisfy the lusts of their flesh. Their words, their dress, and their actions evidence this. This is not to say that we cannot or should not have a good time. In western society, we have little problem having good times. But it should not be to fulfill the lusts of our flesh.

Someone has noted that when a group of Christians wax cold in their love and zeal for the Lord, that their gatherings turn first into big social events. Then they degenerate into downright revelry and become times of celebration of carnal lusts. This is very true of some of the holy days (holidays) that are now celebrated. They have been commercialized or otherwise compromised to become opportunities to let our flesh rule our lives (Christmas, Mardi Gras, etc.).

Any day can be used to honor God or to live for the desires of the flesh. We ought to be careful that our conferences and special meetings do not degenerate into fashion shows, revelry, and opportunities to fulfill the lusts of our flesh.

God judged Manasseh for his wickedness and brought him into prison in Babylon. While in prison Manasseh repented, and God restored him to his throne in Jerusalem (II Chronicles 33:11-13). Manasseh had a true repentance. Once he was back on the throne again, he set out to do that which was right. He destroyed the worship of the false gods and cleansed the house of the Lord. He even commanded his entire nation to serve the Lord.

The weakness he had was that he did not get rid of all the high places. The people as a whole no longer served the gods of the heathen but they still sacrificed in the high places, "yet unto the LORD their God only" (II Chronicles 33:15-17). This was worship of the one true God. But their worship was corrupted worship in that it was not done in the place designated by God for sacrifice.

Whether Manasseh did not remove the high places because of ignorance or choice we do not know. Perhaps he was afraid to bring too much reform to the people. But in leaving the high places standing, he left the door open for backsliding again. As a result, he lost his son's soul to wickedness.

His son Amon was Judah's next ruler. He was an evil king who was even worse than his father had been initially. But Amon refused to humble himself and repent. Consequently, his own servants assassinated him in his own house.

Many Christians today live for God but they fail to destroy the high places. Therefore, their children backslide, being unable to handle the disregard for God's Word. Sometimes, their children never return. We must take care to destroy the high places not only for our own benefit but also considering the future of our children.

We affect our natural children as well as our spiritual children. What road will they travel? What decisions will they make? It is true that what the parents may practice in moderation, the children may take to excess. The strongholds of hell need to be pulled down. The high places must be brought low.

Ministries of the High Places

The next king of Judah was Josiah. He served God like Hezekiah and David. For eight years he went throughout Judah destroying both the images of the pagan gods and the high places in Jerusalem and Judah (II Chronicles 34:2-7, II Kings 23:7-8, 13, 15, 19, and 24). He even did what he could during this time to cleanse part of the land of Israel (the northern ten tribes) from heathen worship. He did this even though that land was under the rulership of the pagans (the Israelites had already been led away captive).

By the time Josiah came to power, wickedness had become so ingrained in the lives of the people that the homosexuals began to form organizations (references to the "houses of the sodomites" in II Kings 23:7). In fact, their organizations were "by the house of the LORD." In other words, they began to exert strong influence in the system of worship to Almighty God. They had taken over some control of the ministry.

> *Some build their ministries from the support of the high places.*

When you think about it, it draws an amazing correlation to our society. Today, there are some churches and organizations where the sodomites are in control enough to where their sin is excused. Too many in the Christian music/entertainment industry are living in adultery, practicing homosexuality, or otherwise sexually violating the laws of God. The influence of homosexuals is felt so strongly in a number of "Christian" churches and organizations that they have gone so far as to declare homosexuals as fit for the ministry. These organizations are nigh to being reprobates according to Romans 1, if they are not already there.

II Kings 23:9 tells us that the priests of the high places would not go up to the altar of the Lord in Jerusalem. Yet they continued partaking of the ministry. Some people build their ministries on the support of the high places. As long as the high places prosper, they will prosper. Therefore, they will fight tooth and nail to keep the high places going strong. It is much like the bureaucrat who will fight to keep his or her agency open when that agency is clearly unprofitable or even counter-productive to the taxpayer. So these ministries of the high places will work to excuse the existence of their high places.

Often, some of those who are involved in the ministry of a church which thrived on "high places" will refuse to go on to truth that God illuminates to His people. They are too proud to admit specific areas of wrong or imperfection. They continue in their ministry but refuse to do what God has commanded. They refuse to tear down the high places that are displeasing to God. Often, they will attack those that do follow God in tearing down the high places. They will accuse them of various improper motives. They do this to help themselves feel justified.

There are whole organizations that have been built on high places. Usually this was done when it was not known that God wanted some of these high places torn down. In His mercy, He blessed them until they could learn more of His ways.

But when that time came, many refused to go "up to the altar of the LORD in Jerusalem." They were not about to leave their profitable, powerful, and prestigious organizations, churches, or ministries which they had built. They could not bear the thought of abandoning their position. Money, fame, popularity, and prestige were more important to them than pleasing God. They counted the praises of men to be of higher value than the praises of God.

So these individuals continue partaking of the ministry by operating their ministries in the high places. They do not move on to the place of full apostolic restoration that God has called the church. They are too comfortable right where they are. Hence, they will fight for the existence and the continual flourishment of the high places.

In spite of Josiah's diligence for a relatively short period of time, the land never was completely cleansed. Judah had become too comfortable in their manner of living. The high places had become part of their culture. II Chronicles 34:3 says that Josiah only "began to purge" the land from all the high places. The work was never finished. Moreover, the period of time from his beginning to destroy the high places to the end of his reign lasted only nineteen years. Then he died. He was unable to change the habits of the people during that period.

It can be a difficult thing to change a culture entrenched in wickedness -- difficult, but not impossible. Jesus said, "With God all things are possible" (Mark 10:27). He said, "I have overcome the world" (John 16:33). The early church often did have an effect on the culture of their converts (Acts 17:6, 19:18-20).

Josiah's son, Jehoahaz, was the next one to come to power in Judah. He was a wicked king, as well was his successor, Jehoiakim (his brother). Jehoiachin was next and was evil as well. Zedekiah, the last king of Judah, was also evil. Throughout their reigns, the high places flourished as did the pagan worship of false gods. During their reigns Judah was taken into captivity. This gives us an overview of the effect of the high places on the children of Judah. And it gives us much to consider.

"Lord Jesus, help us to give diligence to make our calling and election sure that no high places may undermine our faith. Remind us to contend always for the faith, using all our influence to promote righteousness, truth, and your kingdom. Help us to lead a pure lifestyle, walking humbly before you. Keep us from developing alliances with those who would lead us away from the purity of the faith. Help us to build our ministries and churches in purity rather than on the support of the high places. In the holy name of Jesus."

CHAPTER TEN

GOING UP TO THE HIGH PLACES

If we will search the words of the prophets of God to Israel in the Old Testament, we will find that one of His complaints with Israel was that they mixed the holy and the profane, the clean and the unclean. Therefore, their worship became corrupted.

How could do they do such a thing? Where did this happen? Worship of Yahweh (the LORD) was mixed with the worship of the idols in the high places. The purity of worship was in the temple, at least initially (before it was polluted there, too). But the existence of the high places corrupted the true worship of the Lord God. God had one high place where He wanted the people to go to and that was Jerusalem. Our one high place is that of a perfect heart. God wants our complete heart. He wants our complete focus.

When we go up to the high places we must go up with a right heart. When we go up to the high places we must go up to tear the devil's kingdom down. When we interact with the supernatural we must do so with a pure heart. Only when we go up with a right heart can we tear the high places down. If we do not go up with a right heart, then we will go up to the high places to worship. If we do not go up to tear them down, we will end up worshipping there. It is one or the other. We must take care to tear the high places down.

High places are places of worship. They are places of interaction with the spiritual world that are not in line with God's plan. If we visit them without the intention of tearing them down, then we must not kid ourselves into thinking that we will not end up worshipping there.

There have been men of God who have done that which is right. Perhaps they removed all the sodomites and those involved in activities that are morally displeasing to God. They may have even served God with a perfect heart. But they never took down some of the high places.

> *If we do not go up to the high places to tear them down, then we will end up worshipping there instead.*

This is not meant to discredit the good that they have done. Nor is it meant to discredit them as individuals. This is only a warning that if we intend to begin reigning in the spirit, we must be willing to tear the high places down. We must be willing to get rid of all things that are displeasing to God.

Types of High Places

A form (or evidence) of high places is a lack of the fear of God. By this I do not mean being afraid of God. If this were the case we would be afraid even to go to Him to obtain mercy and find grace to help in time of need (Hebrews 4:16). I am referring to possessing a healthy reverence and respect for God and all the things of God.

We in the modern church have often made the sacred things common. Nothing is too sacred to us that we cannot treat it with disrespect. In other words, we have profaned the holy. We often remove any criticism that may come our way for treating the things of God with disrespect by saying that "God has a sense of humor." Indeed He does. But He still desires a distinction between the holy and the profane.

> *A stronghold is a system of destructive thinking.*

It is not uncommon to hear the name of Jesus being taken in vain. We willingly joke about praying in the name of Jesus or use its mention for any trivial (or vain) thing. And when we do not use the name itself, we tend to speak "minced oaths" or slang words that were derived from some mention of God.[11] Hopefully, we have not sunk so far as to use His name as a curse word.

---

[11]Some examples would be "geez" which comes from "Jesus," and "golly" or "gosh" which comes from "God."

There are also those who think it is funny to imitate speaking in tongues or they engage in some other form of playing around with the things of the spirit. This is a dangerous attitude. God is still a jealous God. And He still desires for His people to walk with a fear of God.

Other high places have to do with the lusts of the flesh. Even if there are no acts committed, if the fantasies are worked out in your mind, there is a stronghold there. This stronghold stems from a high place that has developed or that may never have been destroyed. It is a mindset that will work to your ruin or destruction. It is a thought process that leads to sin and self-destruction.

We may see some results when we worship at high places but that does not necessarily signify God's approval. Moses smote the rock when God wanted him to speak to it. The water still flowed but God was not pleased with his action (Numbers 20:7-13). It cost

> *We should be careful not to confuse results of some kind with approval from God.*

him the right to enter the promised land. Balaam was able to prophesy under the influence of the Spirit of God and prophesied correctly but it does not mean that God was pleased with him (Numbers 22:7-9, 22-34, 3-14, et al). We should be careful not to confuse results of some kind with approval from God.

Pagan Influence

Some high places are doctrinal in nature. They are doctrines of men (perhaps even doctrines of devils) that have been handed down to us from days gone by in the form of tradition. Not all traditions are bad. Some are even profitable to us. The problem is that many are traditions of men and not the commandments of God. Even if they are good traditions, when we lift a tradition of man to the level of a commandment of God we have erected a high place (Mark 7:6-9, 13).

Some doctrinal high places are rooted in an unscriptural ritualism. Others go beyond ritualism and entail a corrupted view

> *Paganism is the dividing of the deity of God.*

of God. It is amazing to notice how many in Christianity have a view of God that is not true to the basic form that Scripture gives us. One example of days gone by would be of a God that demands His people to abuse their bodies to try to gain His favor, by doing such things as crawling on broken glass. But we can only approach God on the basis of His mercy, because of Calvary – not our works or goodness. We are justified by faith.

Another example would be the view of God as One who does not care about your sins and that will allow you to live any way you desire to live. This view holds that God is love and, therefore, cannot bring judgment. But the wages of sin has always been death.

Yet another example would be those that possess a multitheistic view of God (more than one God) while the Bible plainly teaches a monotheistic view of God (only one true God -- Deuteronomy 6:4, et al). They view God as several completely separate entities that unite together to make up the Godhead. What this view does is divide the deity of God, which is essentially paganism.

Paganism is the dividing of the deity of God. In the pagan world, they divided the deity of God into many deities. They understood that there was essentially one God. They understood that there was a "God of all gods" who was above every other power. But they still divided up the deity of God.

They would do it like this. They would have a god for the raising of crops. They had a god for success in battle. They had a god for success in a business venture. They had a god for love and a god for healthy childbearing. They had a god for safety in travel. Sometimes they even had gods for various days of the year.

Today, some may do it a little bit differently. They have a saint to help us in the raising of crops. They have a saint for successful business ventures. They have a saint for lost children. They have a saint for safety in travel. They have a saint to help you sell your home. They may even have saints for different days of the year.

It may be argued that a saint is not the same as a god. But truly, any time you pray to someone, you make a god out of him or her. Any time you petition a spiritual being for help, you have made a god out of them.

So we must guard against all high places. We must guard against paganism in any form. We must guard against the heathenistic practice of dividing up the deity of God. We must not allow the high places of the heathen to make inroads to our walk with God or our view of God.

There is only one God who rules the universe (Malachi 2:10). That one God was manifest in the flesh (I Timothy 3:16).

That one God had His own Word to be made flesh (John 1:1, 3,14). That flesh was called the man Christ Jesus.

Any concept of God that violates this basic principle is paganistic in nature. And although God may tolerate some things, it does not mean that He is pleased with it. He still desires all the high places to be torn down.

It may be argued that an improper view of God is not that big a deal as long as you love Him. But our thoughts about God shape

> *Faith is the blood of eternal life. But faith that does not come from God is poisoned blood.*

our lives. Richard Foster has accurately written, "To think rightly about God is, in an important sense, to have everything right. To think wrongly about God is, in an important sense, to have everything wrong."[12]

Part of Jeroboam's problem was that he separated the Godhead. He took the one God of Israel who had delivered them from the bondage of Egypt and made a plurality of beings, placing their likeness in Dan and in Bethel. He also told his followers, "behold thy **gods** [NOTICE THE PLURALITY], which brought thee up out of the land of Egypt" (I Kings 12:28).

Other high places that can be found are in value systems that do not place Jesus Christ at the center. For example, I am all for a positive mental attitude but this cannot be the center of our existence. I am a major believer in faith because faith is the blood of eternal life. But faith that does not come from God is poisoned blood.

Controlling Desires

Another area of high places resides in the lust of the eye and the lust of the flesh. This is shown in the tremendous lack of discipline among some Christians today. They have no true self-control. I am not talking simply about control of anger. I am talking of control over all of our members. I am talking about control of our fleshly desires to the point where they do not rule over us. These lusts are not limited to sexual desires only. They include all the desires and impulses of the carnal nature.

---

12 Richard Foster, 159-160.

We can see this lack of control over the flesh and the self in a number of other examples. One of these would be the prevalence of "impulse shopping" among some Christians today. Another (and related) example is their lack of budgetary control. Their finances and their spending habits are not governed by wisdom. They are governed by the whims of their carnal nature. They are not being good stewards of that which has been placed in their care.

They may go to a store intending only to get certain items but before they leave, they have found numerous other things that have caught their fancy which they do not need. They could not leave the store without purchasing it because they "just had to have it." Then they wonder why they are consistently in financial bondage.

I am not talking about things that they needed or were planning to buy anyway. But by impulse they may buy that candy just to munch on while they are shopping though they are trying to lose weight. They may buy some little gadget that they will never use and sometimes do not even like. Later, they disdain the purchase as foolish spending and regard it as a waste. But at the time they were simply being ruled by the lust of the eye. They are catering to their flesh. They are only looking to satisfy every demand, comfort, and convenience their flesh desires. They are allowing themselves to get stuck in the lower dimensions of life.

More evidence of lack of self-control is in their eating habits. They may be eating at a restaurant somewhere and they will overeat. Perhaps it was an "all-you-can-eat" dinner. Then they complain about how badly they feel because they ate too much. This is simply indulgence. It was their lusts working at the time and controlling their actions. Their flesh demanded to be given space so they obliged. Others manifest this lack of control over the things they watch or listen to.

Now I am not trying to say some of these activities are "heaven or hell." But they can often be strongholds through which Satan works to hinder the plan of God from being worked out in our lives. I am not saying that we should run around living ascetic lifestyles. I enjoy the prosperity that we have in America. But this does not give us an excuse to let our flesh dictate to us. We should not be brought under the control of our lusts. Paul said, "All things are lawful unto me, but all things are not expedient: all things are lawful for me, but I will not be brought under the power of any" (I Corinthians 6:12).

In I Corinthians 10:23 he said it again, "All things are lawful for me but all things are not expedient: all things are lawful for me, but all things edify not." He was not going to allow any desire of the flesh to control his actions. The only thing he would allow to control his actions and decisions was His Lord and Master. Only the Spirit of Christ would be allowed to dictate his life.

In the verse immediately before, he asked the question, "Do we provoke the Lord to jealousy?" Even in our New Testament Age, God is still a jealous God. He can still be provoked to jealousy by those things which may be lawful but are not "expedient" or that do not edify.

We do have a liberty in Christ Jesus where we do not have to live by the letter of the law. I thank God for this freedom. But some use this teaching to promote a

> *Condemnation is not the feeling of guilt. It is the sentence of death passed on to us because of sin in our lives.*

lack of principles by which we should guide our lives. They call this liberty. Truly, we have been called unto liberty. "Only *use* not liberty for an occasion to the flesh" (Galatians 5:13).

The Apostle Peter spoke of these individuals in II Peter 2:10-22. He said that they "walk according to the flesh in the lust of uncleanness." They "count it pleasure to carouse in the daytime" (verse 13).

"For when they speak great swelling *words* of emptiness, they allure through the lusts of the flesh, through lewdness, the ones who have actually escaped from those who live in error.

"While they promise them liberty, they themselves are slaves of corruption; for by whom a person is overcome, by him also he is brought into bondage.

"For if, after they have escaped the pollutions of the world through the knowledge of the Lord and Savior Jesus Christ, they are again entangled in them and overcome, the latter end is worse for them than the beginning.

"For it would have been better for them not to have known the way of righteousness, than having known *it*, to turn from the holy commandment delivered to them.

"But it is happened to them according to the true proverb: 'A dog returns to his own vomit,' and 'a sow, having washed, to her wallowing in the mire'" (II Peter 2:18-22, NKJV).

In Galatians 5:25 Paul said, "If we live in the Spirit, let us also walk in the Spirit." The Greek word behind "walk" comes from the word *stoikeo* which means to advance, to progress, or to frame one's conduct by a certain rule. He told us that if we would walk in the Spirit, we would not fulfill the lusts of the flesh (Galatians 5:16).

Thus, if we are fulfilling the lust of our flesh, then we are not walking in the spirit. If we are not walking in the spirit then condemnation is sure to come our way (Romans 8:1). This is because we will be ruled by the lusts of our flesh, which only brings forth sin, which always brings forth death (James 1:14-15). So we have condemnation. Now condemnation is not the feeling of guilt. Condemnation is the sentence of death passed on to us as a result of sin in our lives.

> *If we are fulfilling the lusts of our flesh, then we are not walking in the spirit.*

That is why Jesus did not come to condemn the world. The world was already condemned because of sin. Jesus came to save. The Holy Ghost does not desire to condemn. He works to convict, to show us our wrong and to lead us to what is right (John 16:7-10, Jude 14-15). Oh, the wonder God's grace! He lifts us up from the miry clay and empowers us to walk on that higher path.

If we are walking in the Spirit, then we will bear the fruit of the Spirit. We will display the evidences of the Spirit at work in our lives. Part of the fruit of the Spirit (or part of the results of truly allowing the Spirit of God to rule our lives) is temperance (Galatians 5:23). Temperance has to do with self-control in all things. It is control of the self. It is much better than just being moderate. It is being temperate.[13]

Corrupted Worship

Sometimes the high places were used to worship the true God but the worship which was offered there was corrupted worship. Sometimes we are guilty of that. We will come to church

---

[13]For more on temperance, see David Sanzo, *The Key to the Kingdom* (Mobile, AL: Companion Press, 1997), 42-45.

to worship God. We end up enjoying the show because we have great music and entertainment. Our focus is more on the music and the beat and the song and the "feel good" feeling than it is on the one true God. This is a high place. It is corrupted (not pure) worship. It is not that we are not allowed to enjoy the music, etc. It is that our focus is to be on God.

"True worshippers will worship the Father" (John 4:23, NKJV). The Father is looking for those who will worship Him. He is looking for the true worshipper because they will worship Him in spirit and in truth. Those who worship Him **must** worship Him in spirit and in truth (John 4:24). It must be a pure worship, a right worship.

In some churches they have resorted to choreographed dancing because they do not have enough of the Spirit of God moving in their midst to where people will do it of their own spontaneous free will. So they come up with a psychological gimmick which makes it someone's job or position to "dance unto the Lord." This way when they dance, they can be excused in the minds of people as "they are supposed to do it." Often, the dancer is not even thinking of worship; they are thinking about the next moves they are going to make. In addition, when the dance is done in a way as to excite sexual lust, it cannot be pure worship.

It gets worse. One noted minister made a revealing remark. He said, "I have spoken to men who have watched choreographed dancing, and they have said that the most pleasure they got out of it was watching women move around sensually."[14] This is not pure worship. This is corrupted worship.

Jesus referred to the corrupted worship of some in His day.

"Hypocrites! Well did Isaiah prophesy about you, saying:

"'These people draw near to Me with their mouth, and honor Me with their lips, but the heart is far from Me.

"'And in vain they worship Me, teaching as doctrines the commandments of men'" (Matthew 15:7-9, NKJV).

Isaiah put it like this:

---

[14]Ron Auch, *Taught by the Spirit*, (Green Forest, AR: New Leaf Press, 1991), 23.

"Therefore the LORD said: 'Inasmuch as these people draw near with their mouths and honor Me with their lips, but have removed their hearts far from Me, and their fear toward Me is taught by the commandment of men" (Isaiah 29:13, NKJV).

We may not be sacrificing to false gods but we are not in the one High Place where God has designed worship to take place. We are using the music or other avenues of worship to worship Jesus Christ but the focus is misdirected. The focus of our attention is on the show, not on Jesus Christ. We are worshipping but we do not have just one altar. We are worshipping at other altars.

Entertainment vs. Joy

Too often in our modern western world we have allowed worldly substitutes to filter in among us to take the place of the things of God. But worldly substitutes can never make up for the life that only God can give. Talented performance can never take the place of a work of God. Human skill is a poor substitute for a move of God's Spirit. Human ability cannot match being anointed by the Holy Ghost.

Sometimes we think we are experiencing joy when in actuality we are simply being entertained. Entertainment is a poor substitute for joy. It can only provide some resemblance of a "good time." It cannot provide the good life that joy brings. Joy comes only from God. Entertainment depends on activities.

| *Entertainment is a poor substitute for joy.* |

Where there is entertainment there is sure to be boredom. This is because entertainment comes from the outside. But joy comes from within. Joy is a fruit that can only be manifested as a result of being connected to the Vine, Jesus Christ.

If we allow ourselves to become preoccupied with entertainment we will find that we are worshipping at other altars rather than the one place God desires us to be. If we go to church dressing in a manner that may entice someone to lust after us, we are worshipping at high places. It may be done in ignorance or it may be done knowingly, but it is still a high place in our lives with which God is not pleased. If we sing, dance, praise, or even preach while desiring people to be impressed with our natural ability to get the attention on us, we are worshipping at high places. We are establishing strongholds for the enemy in our worship to God.

We are to crucify the flesh with its affections and lusts (Galatians 5:24). The focus of our attention in worship is not to be centered on someone who manifests graceful movements or a vocal or musical ability. Instead it ought to be centered on the Spirit of God that seeks to meet with us in our worship. Again, this is not to say that we cannot enjoy good music in our worship of God. But that ought not to be the main thrust or goal of our worship.

God desired Israel to have one place of worship to signify the one way that we are to approach Him in our worship. He was displeased with their high places and corrupted

> *We should not confuse God's tolerance with His stamp of approval.*

worship. Likewise, He is displeased with our high places and corrupted worship. He may seem to tolerate it for a while but we should not conclude that He does not mind our high places and corrupted worship.

We should not mistake God's tolerance of something as His stamp of approval. Just because He is longsuffering with us does not mean that He is pleased with us. Just because God's blessing is present does not mean that all things are well. We may have a blessing from God but we will not be able to enjoy its pleasures to the fullest extent as God intended until we have conquered the enemy within.

Pure Worship

Mark 9:1-10 records the story of Jesus being transfigured on a high mountain. Elijah and Moses appeared there with Him. When Peter saw the wonder of it all, he had an idea. He said, "Master, it is good for us to be here: and let us make three tabernacles; one for thee, and one for Moses, and one for Elias."

But the response from heaven was emphatic. A consuming cloud overshadowed them and the audible voice of God thundered. "This is my beloved son, hear him." Immediately afterwards, they looked around and saw no one except for Jesus. God was not interested in worship from three tabernacles. He was not looking to receive worship in three different formats or persons. Jesus said, "no man cometh unto the Father, but by me" (John 14:6).

What is the way of pure worship? How does God desire us to approach Him? Where is the one High Place that He desires for us to come? Isaiah 57:15 says,

> "For thus saith the high and lofty One that inhabiteth eternity, whose name *is* Holy; I dwell in the high and holy *place*, with him also *that is* of a contrite and humble spirit, to revive the spirit of the humble, and to revive the heart of the contrite ones."

Notice that the high place mentioned here is singular. In this high place, the "high" is twice linked to the "holy." So the one High place where God does desire for us to come is a place of holiness. It is not a place of worldliness. It is a place of separateness from the world, a place of holiness.

And this one High Place which we ought to have is where we worship with a contrite and humble spirit. There, in this singular place alone may we worship "the High and Lofty One that inhabiteth eternity." The true worshipper will worship in spirit and in truth.

> **God is not interested in a divided allegiance.**

God does not accept praise or worship offered in arrogance and pride. He will put it off from Him. And lest we think that He could never refuse an offering or a sacrifice, let us remember that He would not even look at Cain's sacrifice. "God resisteth the proud, but giveth grace unto the humble" (James 4:6, I Peter 5:5). God will hold the proud at arm's length.

Jesus told of a prayer offered by a self-righteous and arrogant man. Because of his arrogance, this man felt he could position himself with God any way he wanted. But Jesus explained that this man never returned home justified because he did not approach God with humility (Luke 18:9-14). So there are some types of worship (corrupted worship) with which God is not pleased. There are some types of worship that He will not accept.

The one High Place of the Almighty God is not a place of corrupted worship. It is a place of purity. Jesus said, "Blessed *are* the pure in heart: for they shall see God" (Matthew 5:8). Purity of heart entails having a single focus. Blessed are those who have a single mindedness, for they shall see God.

God would have one place of worship, that is, one way of worship. And that is with your whole heart. He is not pleased with lip service to Him while the mind or the flesh is traveling some other road. This is part of the reason why we must bring every thought into captivity. It is not just about getting out of the first and second dimensions. It is gaining control over the third and fourth dimensions as well. It is about cleansing ourselves from all filthiness of the flesh and spirit.

Jesus told us that the first and greatest of all the commandments was that we were to love the Lord our God with all our heart, with all our soul, with all our mind, and with all our strength (Mark 12:29-30). He is not interested in a divided allegiance. We cannot serve two masters. We must love Him with all of our heart, soul, mind, and strength.

The one place of pure worship is found in the way of holiness. It is the way of separateness -- separating our focus and attention away from the carnal world and centering it on Him. "Set your affection on things above, not on things on the earth" (Colossians 3:2).

Enemies of Self-denial

Paul exhorted the Philippians to note those which lived as he did and to follow his example. He referred to those who are enemies of the cross of Christ. Notice that he does not say that they are enemies of Christ. He says that they are the enemies of the cross of Christ.

> "Brethren, join in following my example, and note those who so walk, as you have us for a pattern.
> "For many walk, of whom I have told you often, and now tell you even weeping, *that they are* the enemies of the cross of Christ:
> "whose end *is* destruction, whose god *is their* belly, and *whose* glory *is* in their shame -- who set their mind on earthly things" (Philippians 3:17-19, NKJV).

These people are not necessarily against Christ Himself. At least, they may not have consciously set themselves against Him as a person. But they have set themselves against His cross. They do not despise Him – they despise His cross.

Paul is referring to people who live without temperance or discipline. They indulge their flesh. Their god is their belly. They are captives to the desires of their flesh. They take great pride in what ought to be considered their shame.

They have set their minds and affections on earthly things rather than heavenly things. Instead of preaching sacrifice, they preach indulgence. Instead of preaching the denying of self, they preach encouragement to those who cater to fleshly interests.

But the place of pure worship is truly the way of sacrifice. Jesus proclaimed, "Whosoever will come after me, let him deny himself, and take up his cross, and follow me" (Mark 8:34b). He told a rich young ruler, "come, take up the cross, and follow me" (Mark 10:21c). I do not find a mention here about indulging the flesh.

> *They may favor the Christ but they despise His cross.*

I do find where He said, "He who does not take his cross and follow after Me is not worthy of Me" (Matthew 10:38, NKJV). I find where Jesus said, "Whoever does not bear his cross and come after Me cannot be My disciple" (Luke 14:27, NKJV). He went on to say, "So likewise, whoever of you does not forsake all that he has cannot be My disciple" (Luke 14:33, NKJV).

You cannot be a disciple of Jesus Christ without being willing to face the cross. Better than that, we must be willing to bear the cross. Paul told the Galatians, "those *who are* Christ's have crucified the flesh with its passions and desires" (Galatians 5:24, NKJV). If you are not willing to tear down the high places you make yourself an enemy of the cross. If you are not willing to crucify the flesh with its affections and lusts you are not truly Christ's.

Friendship with the world makes you an enemy of God (James 4:4). If you are a friend to the carnal nature you cannot be on good terms with God. A promoter of carnality makes himself an enemy of God. God is not pleased with a builder of high places.

The proper place of a walk with God is the path of humility. It is the practice of walking with a perfect (complete) heart. It is the call to being sold out. The true worshipers will worship God in spirit and in truth (John 4:23). They will worship Him with all that they have and all that there is to them. They will worship Him in true honesty and humility.

The Father seeks such to worship Him. He does not seek out the corrupted worship. He may tolerate it at times but He does not seek it out. However, He does seek out those that will worship Him in spirit and in truth. In fact, there is no other way to truly worship Him. The true worshippers will worship Him in spirit and in truth. That is the one way of worship. "They that worship Him **must** worship *Him* in spirit and in truth" (John 4:24).

One songwriter prayed,

> "Lord, prepare me to be a sanctuary
> "Pure and holy, tried and true.
> "With thanksgiving, I'll be a living
> "sanctuary for You."

Churches of Iniquity

In Hosea 10:5, the prophet made reference to "the calves of Bethaven." In Hosea 10:8, he made reference to "the high places also of Aven, the sin of Israel." Bethaven was originally named Bethel. Bethel was one of the places where Jeroboam had placed his calves for Israel (the northern ten tribes) to worship. Hosea said that these high places where the calves had been placed were the sin of Israel.

In I Kings 12:30, we had already learned that this thing became a sin to Israel. By the time Hosea made his prophecies, the sin had become entrenched in Israel. As a result of this corrupted worship (which was instituted initially for political purposes), Bethel eventually became called Bethaven.

Bethel means "house of God." Bethaven means "house of iniquity." The high places of corrupted worship caused that place to go from being known as the house of God to being called the house of iniquity. One of the best definitions of iniquity that I have ever heard is "self-will." The house of God had been turned into a place of self-will. The house of prayer (and reliance or dependence on God) had been turned into a house of independence from God. It was now a place where you were "free" to do anything you desired to do.

Many churches today were once built to be centers of worship to the one true God. It was where people of prayer would gather together to seek His face. But somewhere along the way things changed. Their high places changed the way they operated. The high places changed their purpose for existing. The high places became strongholds to bind the people of God.

The house of God should always be known as a house of prayer, not a house of social activities. Again, as a point of clarification, let me say that I am not against social activities.

However, they should not be the center of our life. They should not be the focal point of our function.

These groups allowed high places to flourish in their midst (sometimes for political purposes like Jeroboam). As a result of the erection of high places in their churches and denominations, many places that had been formerly known as houses of prayer and the house of God have now become dens of iniquity. They are places where carnal nature and self-will rule. They are no longer Bethels but are now Bethavens.

Jeremiah cried out,

> "Cut off thine hair, *O Jerusalem* [THIS IS A SYMBOL OF GREAT SHAME FOR THE "LADY" OF JERUSALEM OR JUDAH, THE "WIFE" OF GOD], and cast *it* away, and take up a lamentation on high places; for the LORD hath rejected and forsaken the generation of his wrath.
>
> "For the children of Judah have done evil in my sight, saith the LORD: they have set their abominations in the house which is called by my name, to pollute it" (Jeremiah 7:29-30).

When we look at some churches today, we see where they have set their abominations -- in the house of God of all places. This makes their house of worship to become the house of iniquity. When you find anything that the Scriptures declare as abominations being excused and even promoted in the church, you have found abominations being set in the house of God. This pollutes His house. In the eyes of God, that place is no longer called Bethel but Bethaven.

The prophet had already stated:

> "Lift up your eyes to the desolate heights and see: Where have you not lain *with men*? By the road you have sat for them like an Arabian in the wilderness; and you have polluted the land with your harlotries and your wickedness.
>
> **"Therefore the showers have been withheld, and there has been no latter rain**. You have had a harlot's forehead; you refuse to be ashamed [MAY THE LORD HELP US NEVER TO GET TO THE POINT WHERE WE REFUSE TO BE ASHAMED OF SIN].

"...she [THE NORTHERN TEN TRIBES OF ISRAEL]has gone up on every high mountain and under every green tree [EVERY HIGH PLACE], and there played the harlot.

"...I had put her away, and given her a certificate of divorce; yet her treacherous sister Judah did not fear, but went and played the harlot also.

"And yet for all this her treacherous sister **Judah has not turned to Me with her whole heart, but in a pretense** [ONLY IN A SIMULATION OF THE REAL THING, I.E., SHE TURNED TO ME DISHONESTLY], says the LORD" (Jeremiah 3:2-3, 6c, 8b and c, 10, NKJV).

The reason why some places have not seen the latter rain of the Holy Ghost is because of their spiritual harlotries. Sometimes they are so adamant about their ways that they refuse to be ashamed for doing that which displeases God. God gave the northern ten tribes a bill of divorcement, hoping Judah would learn a lesson from it. But the nation of Judah only turned to God superficially. They drew near with their lips but their heart remained far from God.

God is looking for a people that will draw near to Him with their whole heart. He is looking for a people that will tear down the high places of the enemy. He desires to send a revival where we will overcome all of Satan's strongholds whether they are in places like New York, Los Angeles, or Washington, D.C. We can pull the strongholds down even if they are avenues of great influence like universities, the law, media, or Hollywood. Of course, to do this we must be willing to pull down the strongholds within ourselves.

"Great Savior, help us to develop a proper fear (respect) for you and all the things of God. Guide us in tearing down the high places in our lives. Help us to deny ourselves, to crucify the flesh with its desires, to rule over our bodies rather than letting it rule over us. Help us to walk in the spirit. Help us to give you our whole allegiance. Help us never to be enemies of the cross of Christ and to beware of those who are. Help us not to be guilty of making divisions in your deity. Help us to offer pure worship to you. Let your faith work in and through us. Let your joy naturally flow through us. Help us not to settle for any substitutes for your love, joy, and peace. In Jesus' name."

CHAPTER ELEVEN

OUR SOLE REFUGE

"The LORD also will be a refuge for the oppressed, a refuge in times of trouble.

"And they that know thy name will put their trust in thee: for thou LORD, hast not forsaken them that seek thee." -- Psalm 9:9-10.

The Hebrew word behind "refuge" refers to a high place. The Lord Himself is expected to be our high place, our place of security. He is to be our harbor of peace and rest. He is to be our only place of refuge. Our trust is to be in Him alone.

Jeremiah told backsliding Judah, "Truly in the LORD our God *is* the salvation of Israel" (Jeremiah 3:23c). He alone is our salvation. There is only one way of salvation (Acts 4:12). There can only be one place of sacrifice, only one sacrifice in which we have confidence, and that is Calvary.

Hebrews 10 says that there is "no more offering for sin" (verse 18) and "no more sacrifice for sins" (verse 26). There is no other offering or sacrifice. In God alone do we find salvation. No man can come to the Father but by Jesus Christ. The man Christ Jesus is the only mediator between that one true God and men (I Timothy 2:5).

Some would like to turn our attention away from the ransomed work of Jesus Christ, away from His work at Calvary. They pay lip service to it but desire to continue in the ways of the world or after their own will. They still do their own thing. They do not understand that God despises the high places with its corrupted worship.

I Corinthians 10:21 says, "Ye cannot drink the cup of the Lord, and the cup of devils: ye cannot be partakers of the Lord's table, and of the table of devils."   Again, we cannot serve two masters. If we serve the One, we must serve Him as He desires to be served. His first commandment is that we serve no other god but Him (Exodus 20:3). His greatest commandment is that we love Him with all our heart -- free from high places. To serve Him in a manner unacceptable to Him is to serve the other master. We can only serve one or the other.

Overcoming Strongholds or Flashbacks

"(For the weapons of our warfare *are* not carnal, but mighty through God to the pulling down of strongholds;)

"Casting down imaginations, and **every high thing** that exalteth itself against the knowledge of God, and bringing into captivity every thought to the obedience of Christ;

"And having in a readiness to revenge all disobedience, when your obedience is fulfilled" (II Corinthians 10:4-6).

Our minds are private battlegrounds that can be easy prey for the erection of high places. Satan uses these strongholds as a place where fear, unbelief, and depression can rule our lives. These high places promote strongholds for pride, jealousy, and rebellion. Lust, laziness, and immorality can reign from strongholds. Bitterness, unforgiveness, and hatred can spue their venom more effectively from a high place.

Strongholds in our lives could be described as destructive patterns of thinking or systems of thought.   They may not always necessarily be "sin" but it does not diminish the importance of removing

> *Our minds are private battlegrounds that can be easy prey for the erection of high places.*

them from our lives. The high places served as triggers that reminded Israel that they could serve another god, that they could fulfill the lusts of their flesh by serving these other gods. Their high places were really strongholds of the enemy.

Our high places are often discovered in the form of things that trigger our mind to begin contemplating (or worshipping) other systems of thought, other lusts or desires. They can work like the flashbacks many people experience who have suffered through trauma. These strongholds of the enemy trigger us to fall to certain temptations.

When some of the soldiers returned to the United States from fighting in Vietnam, they suffered flashbacks which caused them to think that they were still in Vietnam fighting against the enemy. There were certain words, scenes, or situations that would trigger a flashback in their minds to the battlegrounds in Vietnam. Because they did not fight a war to win it completely, they could not win it completely in their minds. So they were tortured by these flashbacks -- these strongholds in their minds against which they struggled to set themselves free. If we are not wholehearted in our determination to win our spiritual battles, we allow high places to be set up that will trigger flashbacks (which in the spirit are much more real than they are in the flesh).

The enemy takes pleasure in rehearsing to us our past failures and transferring them to the present circumstances. Just because you failed in the past does not mean you are a failure. All it means is that you are not God. Do not let a single failure build such a great stronghold in your life that you become a slave to the enemy's flashbacks.

How High Places Are Built

Romans 1:18 tells us that "the wrath of God is revealed from heaven against all ungodliness and unrighteousness of **men, who hold the truth in unrighteousness**." There are "religious" folks who hold truth but they hold it in unrighteousness. They suppress it in unrighteousness. Against them the wrath of God is unleashed. How did these individuals get to the place that the wrath of God was let loose on them?

It starts with the building of high places. We see the progression beginning in verse twenty-one. It states "that, when they knew God, they glorified *him* not as God.

First of all, the high places are built away from where the glory of the Lord resides. This is where the high places of Israel were built. They built the high places away from the tabernacle of the Lord. In the tabernacle was the place where the ark of the covenant was found. The ark of the covenant was the place where the glory of the Lord rested. Their high places took the focus off of the ark of the covenant and the glory of the Lord.

Usually we build our high places away from God's glory. We start by not focusing on the glory of God. We do not center our attention on His power and all the great things He alone can do. Instead, we concentrate on our own talents and abilities. We fail to glorify God as God. We fail to recognize Him for who He really is.

Even if we do recognize Him for being who He really is, we do not want Him to get the glory for it. Of course, with our mouths we may say that we desire for Him

> **The high places are built away from where the glory of the Lord resides.**

to receive all glory but in our hearts we covet the glory. We desire for men to look at us and marvel at our abilities without pointing them to God. We like to get drunk on the glory. But God said, "I will not give my glory unto another" (Isaiah 48:11).

Paul next said that they became unthankful. This is the result of losing the respect for God's glory. When you lose respect for God's glory, you will not be thankful to Him for His many blessings to you.

Although you cannot be thankful without verbalizing it, you can say "thank you" without being thankful. Thankfulness is not nearly as much a word as it is an attitude. When you are thankful, you will have an attitude of gratitude.

Too many today do not have a heart of gratitude. They can only focus on the negative. The heart of this unthankful spirit is pride. Being thankful is a mark of humility. Instead, the unthankful think they are "entitled" to every privilege available. They have convinced themselves that the world owes them, the church owes them, the preacher owes them, and even their family owes them. They cannot recognize the kindnesses given on their behalf because they see every blessing of good or service as their "right."

The truth is that God owes us nothing. We are in debt to Him. And it would be good to recognize that no one else owes us anything either. With this thought in mind, it is much easier to be thankful. We become grateful for the many kindnesses shown to us. With this mindset, it is much easier to have a servant's heart.

These people first build their high places (their focus of worship) away from the glory of God. This causes them to be lifted up with pride and to become unthankful. Paul then said that the people become vain in their imaginations. The Greek word behind "vain" is *mataio*, which means being devoid of force, truth, success, and result. It refers to that which is futile, groundless, ineffective, useless, fruitless, unprofitable, and empty.[15]

The prophet records God's bewilderment with this mindset: "Has a nation changed *its* gods, which *are* not gods? But my people have changed their Glory for *what* does not profit" (Jeremiah 2:11). When you move away from the glory of God you will follow after vanity, that which does not profit.

> **When you move away from the glory of God you will follow after that which is unprofitable.**

At this point, they become void of power and truth for when your thoughts are full of vanity (emptiness) you become powerless. Their imaginations become unprofitable and empty in the eyes of God. They dwell on thoughts that are ineffective, fruitless, and futile especially in regards to their efforts to deliver people from sin and save their souls. They then become this way (ineffective, fruitless, and futile) in their lives, particularly in regards to doing that which is good, wise, and profitable. They become ineffective against the enemy.

These types of imaginations exalt themselves against God. They lift themselves up to take His place. They take the things they have imagined and exalt them as being equal to or greater than God is. II Corinthians 10:5 teaches us that we should cast down the imaginations that exalt themselves against God.

Diminishing Vision

In following this path to the wrath of God Paul said their foolish heart becomes darkened. At this point, their heart is categorized as foolish. Psalm 14:1 says, "The fool hath said in his heart, `There is no God.' They are corrupt, they have done abominable works, *there is* none that doeth good."

They no longer seek after God. Up until this point, they did continue to seek God. It's just that they sought after other things as well. They sought after God but not with a perfect heart, a pure heart, all of their heart. Now, in their heart they have said that there is no God. What they say with their mouths is of secondary value

---

[15] "Mataio," *The Analytical Greek Lexicon Reviesed*, ed. By Harold K. Moulton, (Grand Rapids, Michigan: Zondervan Publishing House, 1978).

because in their heart they have purposed to live as if there were no God.

Psalm 14:6 says that these fools "have shamed the counsel of the poor, because the LORD *is* his refuge." These people then belittle those that truly trust in the Lord. We surely have those types of "Christians" today. Those who put their trust in the Lord are mocked by them and deemed abnormal.

Subsequent to this, in Romans 1:22, Paul said, "Professing themselves to be wise, they became fools." This is closely related to the previous step. At this point, they develop a strong reliance on their reasoning powers. Now intellectualism becomes their god.

I am not saying that Christianity is antagonistic to reason for that would be false. True and proper reason proves Christianity. But intellectualism is not our god. We do not esteem our own understanding to be supreme.

We recognize that God's ways are higher than our ways and His thoughts are higher than our thoughts (Isaiah 55:8-9). Especially when it comes to understanding spiritual things, we know that "the natural man receiveth not the things of the Spirit of God: for they are foolishness unto him: neither can he know *them*, because they are spiritually discerned" (I Corinthians 2:14). It takes a spiritual mind to understand spiritual things.

This mindset of having intellectualism as god is actually the foundation of the outlook of atheism. They believe their own reasoning powers are so superior to all knowledge and possible future discovery that they can confidently assert that there is no God.

To make this clearer, let me ask you a couple of questions. Have you **ever** met an atheist or agnostic who was not convinced of his or her own brilliance? Have you **ever** met one who thought they were not really all that intelligent? Have you ever talked with an atheist who doubted his or her own reasoning powers or who manifested humility? I dare say not. Arrogance concerning their own mental abilities seems to characterize all who believe there is no God. At the very least, arrogance is found in relation to thoughts about God.

In fact, you could say that intellectual arrogance is necessary to that type of thinking. It is pure arrogance that states there is no God. You would have to be all over the universe at the same time as well as being in every dimension imaginable to make sure of such a bold claim.

My guess is that you will not meet a humble atheist. The two words do not go together. When they reach humility, they will have simultaneously left their atheism. But as long as they are wise in their own conceits, they will cling to their atheism. They profess themselves to be wise when in actuality, they have become fools. They have become fools in light of eternity.

A Form of Glory

Next, Paul said that they would change the glory of God to images of other kinds. The focus here is not on the glory of God but a representation of the glory. They look not at the Creator but at a representation of the Creator. In other words, they begin to look at creation as God.

Just because they do not focus on the glory of God does not mean there is no desire for it whatsoever. It is just that they have a corrupted desire. Therefore, they focus on a representation of the glory of God.

> *We must be careful not to make a high place out of a representation of God's glory.*

Included in this group we find those that now worship the planet earth as their "mother" or "god." They become pantheists and worship the rocks, the trees, the mountains, and the animals. In America, these are easily borne out by both the "tree huggers" and those individuals who raise the status of animals and the like as being higher than the status of humans.

The nation of Judah also traveled this path of focusing on the representation of the glory rather than on God Himself. Hezekiah had to destroy the brazen serpent that God initially had used to heal the children of Israel in the wilderness. He destroyed it because, by the time he came to the throne, Israel was burning incense to it (I Kings 18:4). They were focused on an image of the glory of God. They were looking to a representation of the glory rather than the glory itself.

Some branches of "Christianity" almost make a god out of various representations of glory. One example is the symbol of the cross. I am thankful for what happened at Calvary but it is not God's desire for us to worship a wooden cross. There is nothing inherently powerful or spiritual about carrying a cross around with you (contrary to what may be portrayed in some horror films).

Others have the same ideas about spiritual good luck charms that they carry or wear. God worked through Paul to use handkerchiefs and aprons from his body to heal people from diseases and to cast out demonic spirits (Acts 19:11-12). But he would not at all have approved of turning around and worshipping and praying to the handkerchief or apron. It was only a tool through which God chose to work.

Starting in Romans 1:24, Paul states that God then gave them up to uncleanness. God gave them up to work sexual immorality among themselves. Though this refers to a perverseness of their actions, it is not limited to committing the acts. It includes the justification of the acts and the acceptance of them as being acceptable and even honorable.

When they do this, they are changing the truth of God into a lie. The truth of God states that some things are abominations. But they try to

> *God is always working to subvert our plans to transgress His laws, without violating our free will.*

change what is actually the truth of God to make it into a lie. Abominations are looked at as being alternative cultures, tastes, preferences, orientations, and lifestyles.

Because I often travel across the United States in my ministry, I spend a lot of time in motels. When I am in a motel, I often pray a prayer where I ask God to hinder people staying in the motel from engaging in various sins while I am there (adultery, fornication, homosexuality, and even pornographic movies). I ask Him to cause numerous events to take place where it just does not work out for them to become involved in these extremely destructive activities. I do not doubt that God answers my prayer.

The truth is that God is always working to subvert our plans to transgress His laws without violating our free will. His love is always working to cause us to leave our sinful activities. So the shoplifter decides not to steal because someone walks into the area. The adulterous affair about to begin gets interrupted by a phone call. The pedophile has someone that comes into the room before anything wrong can happen.

God is working to turn us away from sin. We may look at it as a "missed opportunity" but it is God's way of trying to help us realize that what we are doing is wrong. It is the goodness of God that works to hinder us from sinning. It is the goodness of God that works to lead us to repentance.

However, there is a point where God says, "Alright. I will allow them to do what they have determined to do. They have set their hearts in this direction and have purposed to work their own will. I will not always strive with them. I will let them do what they think they want to do. I will allow them to transgress and work iniquity. I will let them have their own way. I will let them be ruled by the lusts of their flesh. I will let them sin and reap the wages of sin – death."

At this point, God gives them up to do what they wanted to do. If they are determined to commit adultery, He will not stop them. If they are determined to live a homosexual lifestyle, He will remove the pangs of a guilty conscience. If they are determined to use drugs that harm the mind and/or body, He will remove the obstacles He has set in place to discourage them.

Because they "changed the glory of the uncorruptible God into an image made like to corruptible man," and because they desire to worship and serve the creature more than the Creator, God gives them up to their uncleanness and to their vile affections. This is the result of their perverting truth and worship. Because of the hardness and blindness of their hearts, God allows them to trap themselves in the lower dimensions, going as low as the first. Up until this point, God is working to hinder them from sinning, from destroying themselves.

God gives them up to uncleanness in the lusts of their own heart. Because they have purposed to walk in the opposite direction of God, God allows them to arrive at their destination. He will honor their free will. Because they glory in their shame and have pleasure in those that participate in shameful deeds with them, God allows them to trap themselves in the first dimension. God gives them up to uncleanness (verse 24), vile passions (verse 26), and gives them over to a reprobate (debased) mind. This way they are free to do things that are shameful.

According to verses twenty-six through thirty-one, this begins with homosexuality and lesbianism. It progresses to include "all unrighteousness, fornication, wickedness," etc. While in this condition, these folks are given over to a reprobate mind. Again, this does not include just committing the acts but also the justification and the defense of these activities.

They have allowed themselves to be trapped into the captivity of the first dimension. Their will now works against them to keep them there. When people allow the enemy's strongholds to be built in their lives, their lives will end in total destruction (if left unchecked). Truly, if you give the devil an inch, he will take a mile.

But there is hope. There is a way to completely annihilate the devil. It only requires everything you have. I am not talking about your possessions. I am talking about your complete will. I am talking about a real fight -- not fighting just to say that you have fought, but fighting to win. You must be willing to win a complete victory.

"Lord Jesus, give us eyes to see and ears to hear. Help us not to be distracted with following after the many vanities of this world. Remind us to be thankful – not just in word, but also in deed. Most importantly, help us to be thankful in attitude. Help us to focus on your glory. Help us to be changed into that glory. In the most wonderful name of Jesus."

CHAPTER TWELVE

CAGE MATCH

"We wrestle not against flesh and blood, but against principalities, against powers, against the rulers of the darkness of this world, against spiritual wickedness in high *places*" (Ephesians 6:12).

The Greek word behind "wrestle" is an athletic term which is described by Thayer as follows:

"A contest between two in which each endeavors to throw the other, and which is decided when the victor is able to press and hold down his prostrate antagonist, namely, hold him down with his hand upon his neck."[16]

In this contest, you were required not only to pin your opponent to the ground but also have your hand on his neck. This signaled your total dominion over your opponent. In their contests, their policy was "anything goes." The loser in a Greek wrestling match had his eyes gouged out with resulting blindness for the rest of his days.

They offered quite an incentive to give your best in the wrestling match. Who would want to go through life not only having the blemish of a loss on your record but also having lost the privilege of sight for the rest of your life? This would not only be debilitating but it would forever remind you of the shame.

---

[16]Wvest's Word Studies, by Kenneth S. Wvest, 1953, Eerdmann's Publishing Company, Grand Rapids, MI 49502, vol. 1, pg. 141.

The war in which we are involved is for high stakes. This is a "no holds barred" match. We are not simply playing spiritual games. There are permanent consequences related to how we fare in this battle. Both our rewards and our consequences are eternal. Should we lose this fight, we are talking about a permanent loss of sight. We are talking about eternity in the outer darkness.

Habakkuk 3:19 says, "The LORD God *is* my strength, and he will make my feet like hinds' *feet*, and he will make me to walk upon mine high places." We each have our own high places over which we must gain control. We each have our own high places which we must tear down and over which we must gain dominion. The promise that we have from Scripture is that God is our strength. With God as our strength, He will enable us to walk or exercise complete dominion over our high places.

Killer's Instinct

In overcoming problems, we need to have what is known as "a killer's instinct." Let us view the scene where a tan figure is sitting still in the tall desert grass. After a brief moment, it slowly begins to slither into position towards a black and white striped beast who is peacefully grazing to its content. Notice that the animal is not engulfed in a panic driven terror because of the danger nearby. The zebra has been lulled into a false sense of security. It believes all is well.

Suddenly, the lioness leaps from her crouched position towards her prey. The frightened zebra now reacts with a quick jump. Then the striped mammal breaks into a panic run. In a flash of lightning the wildcat is side by side with the animal.

There is only an abbreviated moment in which to take advantage of the situation in order to return to her cubs with dinner. Using her killer's instinct, the lioness does not stumble with hesitation. She quickly sinks her teeth into the zebra's neck. She gives it a short, quick jerk. The zebra falls to the ground. Blood oozes out. The zebra lays there motionless. The hunt has been a success. Dinner is ready.

In war, you must be able to sense when your enemy is at his weakest point. You must understand when he is most vulnerable. If you will act then, before he is able to retreat and renew his strength, you will extinguish him so that he will not be able to rise again and destroy you. You must make your move before he regroups. This is having a killer's instinct. It is not just having the ability to deliver a knockout punch but being mentally strong enough to use that ability at the appropriate time.

> *The killer's instinct is being able and willing to act resolutely at the right moment in order to triumph.*

In sports games, you must know when your opponent is weak mentally and is ready to give up play. If you are a true champion (both of body and of mind) you will sense when they are on the verge of giving up any hope of winning. You will recognize when they are at the point of collapse. If you will be sure to make your move and score at those critical points, you will "break their back." You will eliminate the chances of a successful comeback.

If they get a second wind, it may cause your victory to slip through your fingers. You may lose what you once thought you had already won. But if you will put the game away when you have the chance, you will ensure victory. Acting at that crucial moment is using the killer's instinct.

In the boxing arena, you must know when your opponent is defenseless or is not able to withstand another blow. If you will move in at this critical time, you will knock him out and thus secure the victory. You must be able to deliver the knockout punch. This is the killer's instinct. It is using right timing to take advantage of an opportunity for maximum results. It is solidifying a victory.

If you do not have the killer's instinct and thus fail to act at the point of your enemy's weakest moment, they will survive the round. Then you will have to fight hard again just to bring them to that same critical point where you can knock them out. Of course, there is no guarantee that you can do this a second time. They may gain new life once they escape. They may have survived that round only to come back in a later round to knock you out. This is the importance of the killer's instinct. When you are able to "put it away" you must do so. You must be sure to secure the victory.

Partial Victories

God wants His people to fight against the enemy with a "killer's instinct." According to II Kings 13:14-19, when Elisha was old and getting ready to die, Joash, the king of Israel (not to be confused with the king of Judah also named "Joash"), came to him and wept over the great prophet.

The Scriptures categorize Joash as a wicked king. Even so, he was still influenced by the Spirit of God. He was a "church attender." When he was moved by the prophet while in his presence, God rewarded him. No matter our spiritual condition, when we pay respect to the man of God and seek him out, God will be merciful and reward us.

Elisha told him to get his bow and to shoot his arrows out of the window. This signified the arrow of the LORD's deliverance from the Syrians. Then the prophet told the king to hit the ground with the arrows. Joash responded by hitting the earth three times.

At this point, Elisha became infuriated. He told the king that he should have hit the earth five or six times so that he could totally annihilate his enemy. But since he did not give it his best, he would only win three battles against the Syrians (once for each time he hit the earth). He would not be able to destroy them completely.

Joash knew that Elisha was prophesying to him. He knew that the prophet was giving him a promise. He also knew that the promise was concerning deliverance from Syria. But he still responded haphazardly. He was not working with a killer's instinct. His attitude was careless and indifferent. Therefore, he was not able to break the yoke of bondage totally. He was not able to act with the killer's instinct because his will was not unified. There were too many high places in his life.

Whether you are fighting the enemy of your soul or the lust of your flesh, you must learn to exercise the killer's instinct. There does come a point when you can deliver the "knockout blow" to whatever it is you are trying to conquer.

Remember, we are in a serious battle. The consequences of losing the match may result in permanent blindness. We are not simply trying to survive the round. We are fighting for our souls. We are fighting for the souls of our children. We are fighting for the souls of others. We are fighting for the soul of the city, state, and nation in which we live. We want to defeat the enemy by knocking him out. We dare not wait to secure the victory in some future battle. The stakes are too high.

Praying through – Complete Victory

There is an old-fashioned Pentecostal term used to describe gaining a complete victory over our enemy. It is called "praying through." If some people would just "pray through," they would eliminate the need for much of their counseling.

Yes, I do understand the value of trained counselors to help us in certain situations. But many times people are simply taking up the counselor's time because they do not want to deal with the flesh and crucify it. They refuse to get into their prayer closets like some of the old-timers did and "pray through."

> *Too many times we only win a temporary victory at the altar.*

We need to learn to "pray through" many of our problems. When you "pray through" your problems, you will obtain a victory that cannot be taken away from you. You will "knock out" the enemy because you have determined to use the killer's instinct. You triumph in a way that is more than just temporary.

Too many times we win a temporary victory at the altar. We may feel okay for a night or so but the battle has not been fought to a finish. Some people quit fighting when they do not feel the immediate presence of the enemy. They relax because they feel they have won. But what they do not realize is that their enemy has simply gone into retreat and is hiding. He is cutting his losses short. He is trying to regroup. If they do not keep up the pressure until the enemy is totally defeated, their enemy will live to fight another day.

Then, they will have to pray concerning the same problem over and over again. They will continually be fighting the same battle because they have never put their enemy's lights out. They have to continue fighting the same opponent round after round, never advancing to greater victories. Sometimes the enemy devours them. If they would just get in touch with their killer's instinct, they could knock him out for good.

But to have a killer's instinct, you cannot be double minded. You must understand your purpose and follow it wholeheartedly. If you are not determined to win the battle completely, you will probably eventually lose it completely. The high places will work to divide your will, your desire, your heart, and your mind. This is why we must destroy the high places. We must not be doubleminded for the doubleminded have no promise from God.

Part of our problem in Vietnam was that we fought without exercising the killer's instinct. We would take a hill one day and give it back to the enemy the next. We had numerous opportunities to bring the war to an end victoriously but we held back. Political games were played to the detriment of our soldiers.

This type of thinking destroyed the men we sent there. Many became double minded. They were no longer concerned with defeating the enemy and winning the war. They now began pursuing drugs, alcohol, sex, and various other pleasures. It came back to haunt our soldiers and our whole nation. If we allow ourselves to get double minded in our walk with God, our other pursuits will come back to haunt us.

When the United States fought the Gulf War with Saddam Hussein's regime in 1991, they won an overwhelming victory. But when

> *The doubleminded have no promise from God.*

they had a chance to deliver a knockout blow and defeat Saddam Hussein permanently, they failed to do so. It was not that they did not have the ability to do so. There was no doubt to the Americans' ability. But they did not do so for political reasons. They did not exercise their killer's instinct. As a result, Saddam Hussein has continued to be a thorn in their side on the world scene.

The question is not about our ability. Scripture plainly tells us, "Greater is he that is in you, than he that is in the world" (I John 4:4b). "Whatever is born of God overcomes the world" (I John 5:4a, NKJV). Jesus has given us the right to destroy the works of the devil. "Behold, I give unto you power to tread on serpents and scorpions, and over all the power of the enemy: and nothing shall by any means hurt you" (Luke 10:19). Paul said, "I can do all things through Christ who strengthens me"(Philippians 4:13, NKJV).

Paul explained that God was able to do far above all that we ask or think "according to the power that works in us" (Ephesians 3:20). The question is not about our ability. It is about our resolve to use it. It is about our determination to let the power work in us.

What about your resolve to use the power of God to accomplish the will of God? Is your spirit united? Is it united in its love for God? How focused are you spiritually? Are you ready to win the battle? Are you prepared in your heart to deliver the knockout blow? Do you use your killer's instinct?

"Lord God, help us not to be double minded in our desire for you. Remind us to concentrate our focus in our spiritual journey. Help us to exercise the killer's instinct against the enemy of our souls that we may win a complete victory. Help us not to be intimidated by our enemy. And help us regularly to `pray through.' In Jesus' name."

CHAPTER THIRTEEN

DOMINION OVER HIGH PLACES

In Psalm 18:1, David said, "I will love thee, O LORD, my strength." So whatever is spoken of in the remainder of the psalm rests on the foundation of this statement. Everything that is described afterwards is framed within the context of David loving the Lord and the Lord being David's strength.

In Psalm 18:33, David went on to pray, "He maketh my feet like hinds' *feet*, and setteth me upon my high places." This is exactly what the prophet Habakkuk said. "The LORD God *is* my strength, and he will make my feet like hinds' *feet*, and he will make me to walk upon mine high places" (Habakkuk 3:19). First, he recognized the Lord as his strength. Then God made him to walk on his high places. Once David and Habakkuk made the Lord their strength, He gave them dominion over all their high places.

If we will but truly make God our strength and come to where we rely on Him, He will help us to exercise complete dominion over our high places. Those things that trigger the work of the enemy in our lives will lose their effectiveness against us. When we are possessing our high places or taking complete control over all our high places, the enemy is not able to rise up against us. He will have no stronghold in our lives.

Jesus said, "The prince of this world cometh, and hath nothing in me" (John 14:30). There was nothing in Jesus' life that gave the devil a stronghold in His life. All the high places were destroyed. When we destroy all the high places in our lives, we do not worry about Satan's strongholds against us. Without high places, he is defeated permanently. He is banished to empty darkness. We have knocked him out because we have operated using the killer's instinct.

When one nation seeks to overthrow another, they will use every spy, every organization, every plot of ground which they possess in the enemy's territory, and every device they have at their disposal which they deem necessary or helpful to achieve their goal. What is usually most valuable are the people and places within the enemy's borders that will betray their own country and work with the invaders. It is very difficult to overthrow and subdue a nation that is united. The Romans found this out when trying to rule the British. The British found this out when they tried to rule the Irish.

When Satan seeks to destroy a person, he utilizes the strongholds that he has in that person's life. He cannot overcome us if our eye is single.

> **When we destroy all the high places in our lives, Satan is defeated permanently.**

He cannot succeed if our heart is pure. In the legendary stories of the search for the Holy Grail, Sir Galahad remarks, "My strength is as the strength of ten because my heart is pure." If our heart is pure, there are no strongholds from which the enemy can weaken our resolve to do the will of God. If our focus is not fragmented and our will is not splintered, he will fail. But if we are double minded, he gains a foothold in our lives.

We cannot afford to try serving two masters. What Satan uses to divide our allegiance and to bring us down are the high places in our lives. They are his strongholds. "Let the words of my mouth and the meditation of my heart Be acceptable in Your sight, O LORD, my strength and my Redeemer" (Psalm 19:14, NKJV).

"Lord, let the framework of my thoughts be reconstructed under the guidance of the Spirit of God. Let them be pleasing in Your sight. Help me to think thoughts that are true, honest, just, pure, lovely, of good report, virtue producing, and praiseworthy. Help me cast down evil imaginations, arguments, and every high thing that exalts itself against the knowledge of God. Help me bring every thought into captivity to the obedience of Christ. Help me to destroy the high places, to pull down Satan's strongholds. In Jesus' name, let it be done."

David went on to show the relationship between his being set over his high places and the complete destruction of his enemies. He said in verses 37-38,

"I have pursued mine enemies, and overtaken them: **neither did I turn again till they were consumed.**

"I have wounded them that they were not able to rise: they are fallen under my feet."

David refused to back off the enemy just because they were no longer in his presence. He determined to pursue them until they were consumed. He was in touch with the killer's instinct. He was able to defeat the enemy so badly that they were not able to rise again. David won a complete victory over his enemies. He then exercised a total dominion over them.

Why was David able to totally annihilate his enemies?

"For thou hast girded me with strength unto the battle: thou hast subdued under me those that rose up against me.
"Thou hast also given me the necks of mine enemies; that I might destroy them that hate me" (Psalm 18:39-40).

David reiterated that the LORD was his strength. Therefore, he won such a complete victory over the enemy that he had his hand on their necks. He exercised complete dominion over them.

We need to pursue our enemies in battle until we overtake them running away. We must destroy them. Then, in our wrestling match, God will give us their necks. We will have total victory that will last.

The Aura of Invincibility

In the sports domain, some teams or some boxing champions are said to have an "aura of invincibility." Nobody seems to be able to defeat them. When challengers play them, it seems that the challengers are only trying to see how long they can last or how close they can keep the score. Even they do not believe in their hearts that they can win against the champions. They may hope for the best but they do not truly believe.

I have often noticed that when the champion is shrouded in this cloak known as the aura of invincibility, the challenger will often miss opportunities afforded them. Therefore, they fail to grab the hand of victory when it is presented to them. Instead they get kicked with the foot of defeat. They may or may not realize it but they actually have an opportunity to secure the victory. However, their weakness is they are not mentally prepared for the opportunity.

A lot of times we hear preaching that is designed to help us believe in our hearts that we can overcome through the blood of the Lamb and the

> **When a challenger is not mentally prepared within himself for victory, he becomes a slave to the champion's reputation.**

Word of our testimony (Revelation 12:11). Some preaching is designed to help us understand that we can do all things through Christ who strengthens us (Philippians 4:13). Some preaching is designed to help us become mentally prepared to win a victory. It is designed to help us get our whole will focused into victory, into pleasing God. We need to be prepared to win the battle against our flesh and against the devil.

When a challenger is not mentally prepared within himself for victory, he becomes a slave to the champion's reputation. They begin to fear his roar. The champion's aura of invincibility blinds them. When you carry an aura of invincibility, it will hide your moments of weakness.

I know that in the career of the boxer known as "Iron" Mike Tyson, who has been one of the more effective fighters in the modern era, he carried (at least for a time) an aura of invincibility with him. It seemed that when other fighters entered into the ring with him, they fought only to see how long they could last in a boxing bout with him. It did not appear that they were fighting to win. Therefore, they lost touch with the killer's instinct. Consequently, they were not able to take advantage of his moments of weakness and beat him.

There were several fights where the opponent had rocked him with a punch or had him bouncing off the ropes. They needed only to respond with a killer's instinct to pull off the upset and defeat the champion. But because they believed in Tyson's invincibility, they could not recognize his moment of weakness quickly enough. Consequently, Iron Mike would survive the round and return later in the fight to gain the victory.

Mike Tyson, on the other hand, was in touch with his killer's instinct. He would not let his opponent off the ropes if he knew he had him in his moment of weakness. On the other side of the fight, because his opponents were often intimidated by him (though they never said so publicly, you could tell by their actions in the ring), his opponents could not finish him off when he was in his moments of weakness.

Eventually, a fighter came along who saw right through Tyson's aura of invincibility. When Evander Holyfield had to fight Tyson, he knew the key to beating him was to challenge him in his weakness. He saw through Tyson's appearance of invincibility and came away victorious.[17]

The devil will sometimes cloak your problem with an aura of invincibility. He will tell you that "You can't overcome this problem. You will always be this way. You cannot overcome this weakness. You will always struggle with the past." The devil will tell you that you cannot defeat him. He will try to convince you that he is too strong for you. You will hear whispers saying that you are too weak. They will suggest that the battle is too hard, the journey is too long, and you are too weak or too tired. He will try to persuade you that the sacrifice is too great.

Your enemy will remind you of scriptures just like he reminded Jesus of scriptures. Only he will use the scriptures to try to put you in fear in order to work your destruction. He will remind you that he is described as one who "walks about like a roaring lion, seeking whom he may devour" (II Peter 5:8, NKJV). He wants you captivated by his roar. He will laugh at your efforts to free yourself.

He knows you cannot succeed unless you make the LORD your strength. He wants you to feel that it is useless to keep on trying. So he gets you to focus only on your own strength and its severe limitations. Better yet, he wants you to focus on your weaknesses. He determines to play the video of your past failures so you understand that you cannot overcome. He wants you to see the great victories he has won in the past against you and even against others. He wants you to focus on his aura of invincibility. If he is able, he uses your will to fight against you. He is able to reverse the power of your will if he has high places in your spirit.

Strip Your Enemy Down

In modern boxing matches, the champion will often strut to the ring in expensive, glamorous clothing. They come wearing their championship belts. The announcer is sure to tell everyone of their record, their knockouts, and their titles. But they cannot use any of

---

[17] Though he was the second to defeat Tyson in a professional boxing match, his win was the first that was not considered a fluke by many.

that in the ring. They must be stripped of all of that. Their hope is that their opponents will never strip them of their titles in their minds. But for their opponents to win, they must see the champion stripped of all of their glory.

So you have got to see Satan for who he is. You must see him without the cloak of power and the princely robes in which he likes to parade himself. He gloats in covering himself with a shroud of invincibility. You must understand that the championship belts and the great trophies that he may have won cannot help him in his fight against you. You must dismiss from your mind all the newspaper articles that have been written extolling his greatness.

He cannot take that stuff with him into the ring. Just because he has won a battle against someone else does not mean he is destined to defeat you. Even if he has whipped you before, it does not mean that it has been determined for him to whip you again.

Strip him down and see him for who he is. You can overcome. The prophet Isaiah saw Satan stripped down.

"All they shall speak and say unto thee, 'Art thou also become weak as we? Art thou become like unto us?

"'Thy pomp is brought down to the grave, *and* the noise of thy viols: the worm is spread under thee, and the worms cover thee.

"'How art thou fallen from heaven, O Lucifer, son of the morning! *How* art thou cut down to the ground, which didst weaken the nations!'

"...thou shalt be brought down to hell, to the sides of the pit.

"They that see thee shall narrowly look upon thee, *and* consider thee, *saying*, 'Is this the man that made the earth to tremble, that did shake kingdoms;

"*That* made the world as a wilderness, and destroyed the cities thereof; *that* opened not the house of his prisoners?" (Isaiah 14:10-12, 15-17).

Satan refuses to open the house of his prisoners. It is not because of his great power that he refuses. It is because the prisoners allowed him to establish strongholds in their lives. They permit him to continue to maintain those strongholds. He uses those strongholds to control their will. Therefore, they became captives. And they remain captives. His strongholds in their wills keep them captive even though Satan was defeated long ago by Jesus Christ.

> *The high places residing within their walls keep them captive to a devil that was defeated long ago.*

This is the battle we fight. It is not because Satan is so powerful that he has toppled many. It is because they refused to destroy the high places. They granted him his strongholds.

Jesus has stripped all our enemies of their aura of invincibility. He did it so completely that Paul said, "Having disarmed principalities and powers, He [JESUS] made a public spectacle of them, triumphing over them in it" (Colossians 2:15). The reason why Jesus came was to destroy all of Satan's works (I John 3:8, Hebrews 2:14-15).

Satan cannot take all of his trophies and past victories into the ring with him. He cannot take great glory and power into the ring. But you are allowed to take Jesus into the ring with you. You are permitted to do as both David and Habakkuk did. You are allowed to make the Lord your strength for the battle. You are not prohibited from saying as Paul did, "I can do all things through Christ **which strengtheneth me**" (Philippians 4:13). As a child of God who has been born of the water and of the Spirit, you have been authorized to access His power. You can use His name.

Destined to Win

You have been destined to win. "For whatsoever is born of God overcometh the world" (I John 5:4). This is why Paul could say that we are more than conquerors while we are still involved in wrestling against principalities, powers, the rulers of the darkness of this world, and spiritual wickedness in high places. We are "more than conquerors" (meaning super conquerors) through Him that loved us (Romans 8:37). We are overcomers.

We have been authorized to use His power to triumph over our enemies, just like David and Habakkuk did. Jesus said, "Behold, I give unto you power to tread on serpents and scorpions, and over all the power of the enemy: and nothing shall by any means hurt you" (Luke 10:19).

Serpents have to do with witchcraft. In Acts 16:16, a damsel is described as having a spirit of divination. This phrase can also be translated as having a spirit of Python. In the spirit world, snakes or serpents often have to do with witchcraft.

Scorpions refer to spirits that sting us in our daily lives, unrelated to witchcraft. These spirits antagonize us through the lusts of our flesh and our human weaknesses. These spirits do not necessarily have to be demonic. Scorpions can refer to the wicked human spirits of those who seek our destruction. These spirits (scorpions) will often also provoke us to rebellion (Ezekiel 2:6-7).

But we have been given authority over all of Satan's power. We can destroy serpents, scorpions, and all the power of the enemy in our lives. We can triumph against all the weapons of the enemy. "No weapon that is formed against thee shall prosper" (Isaiah 54:17). No matter what the devil may use to try to bring us down, we can overcome him.

David continues in Psalm 18, .

"Then I beat them as fine as the dust before the wind; I cast them out like dirt in the streets [WOW! CAN WE HAVE TOTAL VICTORY OR WHAT!].

"You have delivered me from the strivings of the people [THESE WERE SOME OF THE SCORPIONS THAT FOUGHT AGAINST DAVID]; You have made me the head of the nations; A people I have not known shall serve me.

"As soon as they hear of me they obey me; The foreigners submit to me.

"The foreigners fade away, and come frightened from their hideouts [THE ENEMY DOES TRY TO HIDE WHEN HE REALIZES YOU ARE WINNING THE BATTLE].

"The LORD lives! [NOW IS THE TIME TO PRAISE THE LORD. NOW IS THE TIME TO CELEBRATE.] Blessed be my Rock! Let the God of my salvation be exalted.

"*It is* God who avenges me, and subdues the peoples under me;

"He delivers me from my enemies. You also lift me up above those who rise against me; You have delivered me from the violent man [MORE SCORPIONS ATTACKING HIS LIFE]" (verses 42-48, NKJV).

David is talking about possessing complete victory. His enemies are totally defeated. He can exercise dominion.

Some who deal in witchcraft have tried to use their spells against the church of Jesus Christ. They have chanted their chants, summoned their demons, and carried out their attacks. They have breathed out their threats and have spit their flames. They have shot their fiery darts.

But we have a promise that we can stand on. "Nothing shall by any means hurt you" (Luke 10:19). I have been told by some who have dealt in witchcraft that said that their curses and spells could not work on someone who had taken on the name of Jesus Christ in baptism and was filled with His Spirit. We have authority over serpents -- if we will use it.

We have authority over other spirits that would desire to work our destruction. They cannot bring us down if we will trust in the Lord. They cannot triumph over us if we make the Lord our strength. We have been granted authority over scorpions -- if we will use it.

Worldwide Dominion

The truth is that we have authority over **all** the power of the enemy. That tells me that not only can we exercise authority over the high places of our own lives, but we can also exercise authority over all the high places (the strongholds) of the enemy. We can tread on the high places of the earth.

Notice what the prophet said in Amos 4:13:

"For, lo, he that formeth the mountains, and createth the wind, and declareth unto man what *is* his thought, that maketh the morning darkness, and **treadeth upon the high places of the earth**, The LORD, The God of hosts, *is* his name."

This makes me want to have a Holy Ghost fit. The reason we are able to exercise complete dominion over the high places of the earth is because the One whom we have made our strength is the One who continually treads on the high places of the earth.

The prophet Micah prophesied, "For behold, the LORD cometh forth out of his place, and will come down, and **tread upon the high places of the earth**" (Micah 1:3). God desires to destroy the high places of the earth so that there will remain only one true High Place.

We can destroy the high places of the earth if we will move in the confidence of the Holy Ghost. We can pray a prophetic prayer that says, "Satan, I have made the Lord to be my strength. In the name of Jesus Christ I rebuke you and your work in my life. tear down your high places. I destroy all your strongholds. I will not be held captive to your thinking. I will not be a slave to the desires of my carnal nature or to your lies. I will serve the Lord alone. He is my strength."

We can tread on the high places of corrupted worship. We can tread on the high places where the enemy builds his military fortifications or strongholds. We do not have to be haunted by our enemy. We can gain total victory. David gained complete victory. He had dominion over the high places of the earth. He said, "You have made me the head of the nations" (Psalm 18:43).

The question is, Where is your confidence? Where is your spiritual strength? From which source do you gain your strength? How do you renew your strength? Is it in the Lord God alone or is your confidence in some other high place? Could it be in your own works of righteousness or holiness? Is your strength in the pride of your own abilities rather than the humility of relying solely on God?

Moses said,

"Happy *art* thou, O Israel: who *is* like unto thee, O people saved by the LORD, the shield of thy help, and who *is* the sword of thy excellency! and thine enemies shall be found liars unto thee; and **thou shalt tread upon their high places**" (Duet 33:29).

The people whom the Lord saves and who have Him as their sword and shield in battle are promised that they will tread on the high places of their enemies. All of their enemies' prophecies will fall to the ground. Their enemies will be found liars unto them.

Oh, let us put on the whole armor of God! Take up the shield of faith! Let your confidence rest in the Lord for He is ever the Almighty. Make Him your strength. He has no competition. He knows no equal. Thrust through your enemy with the sword of the spirit. Speak the Word of God!

Isaiah 66:1 records God as saying, "The heaven *is* my throne, and the earth *is* my footstool." We are talking about a God who is higher than any high place. He is "higher" than any stronghold the enemy may construct. He rules from heaven. The universe is where He sits to rule all else. The earth is under His dominion.

We are able to have dominion over all high places. Our dominion is not limited just to our own high places (Habakkuk 3:19). It also includes the high places of the enemy .

The Blessings of Dominion

Deuteronomy 32:12-14 shows us that when we ride on the high places of the earth with God, He will give us many great blessings. Israel was led out of Egypt and made to ride the high places of the earth. It says,

> "the LORD alone did lead him [REFERRING TO ISRAEL], and *there was* no strange god with him.
> "He made him ride on the high places of the earth, that he might eat the increase of the fields; and he made him to suck honey out of the rock, and oil out of the flinty rock;
> "Butter of kine, and milk of sheep, with fat of lambs, and rams of the breed of Bashan, and goats, with the fat of kidneys of wheat; and thou didst drink the pure blood of the grape."

The Lord made Israel to ride on the high places of the earth. This goes beyond just having total dominion over our own high places. We can have dominion over the high places of the earth, over Satan's entire kingdom. God did this for Israel.

I know that this is talking about the nation of Israel in Moses' day. But there is yet a type here of us having dominion. The definition of "Israel" refers to one who has power with God. Those who have power with God may ride with Him on the high places of the earth. To them belongs total dominion over all the works and manifestations of the devil's kingdom.

Notice that he said that it was the Lord alone who was with the people of Israel. They were not serving other gods. There were no strange gods with him. The LORD was God alone.

When we learn to make the Lord alone to be God, not allowing any strange gods in our lives, then we can ride on the high places of the earth. When we learn to live without any high places where we can offer corrupted worship, then the blessings connected with having dominion over the high places will be ours.

Among other things, these blessings include financial blessings (the increase of the fields); the miraculous (honey out of the rock); and industry, productivity, fruitfulness, or the evidence of the hand of God (oil out of the flinty rock); and physical health (butter and milk). It also includes the desires of our hearts.

Remember that the natural world is a picture of the spiritual world. What great blessings are ours when we rule over the high places.

In Isaiah 58:13-14, God told Israel,

"If thou turn away thy foot from the sabbath, *from* doing thy pleasure on my holy day; and call the sabbath a delight, the holy of the LORD, honorable; and shalt honor him, not doing thine own ways, nor finding thine own pleasure, nor speaking *thine own* words:

"Then shalt thou delight thyself in the LORD; and I will cause thee to ride upon the high places of the earth, and feed thee with the heritage of Jacob thy father: for the mouth of the LORD hath spoken *it*."

We know that our sabbath in the age of the New Testament Church is the Holy Ghost. Isaiah prophesied concerning the Holy Ghost saying, "For with stammering lips and another tongue will he speak to this people. To whom he said, This *is* the rest *wherewith* ye may cause the weary to rest; and this *is* the refreshing" (Isaiah 28:11-12). The Holy Ghost is our rest.

Jesus, who was introduced as the One who would baptize with the Holy Ghost, said, "Come unto me, all *ye* that labor and are heavy laden, and I will give you rest" (Matthew 11:28).

Now the prophet said that if we would call our sabbath a delight, then some things would happen. He said that we were to call it the **holy** of the Lord. Again, the one High Place is to be a holy place. It is not a place of worldliness. Neither is it a weary burden. It is a delight.

He said to call our sabbath honorable. We are to honor God by not doing our own thing or pleasure. We do not indulge in our own high places. We are not to work our own will (iniquity). And we are not to speak our own words. We are to speak the words of our sabbath, the words of our rest, the words of the Holy Ghost.

He said that if we would do this, THEN we would be delighting ourselves in the Lord. The results of delighting ourselves in the Lord is that He will cause us to **ride on the high places of the earth**. This means that we get the blessings connected with riding the high places of the earth. Isaiah said that these blessings included God feeding us with the heritage of Jacob.

Riding on the high places of the earth seems to me to be even greater than simply walking on them. We are riding in God's fiery chariot over them. We do not even need to let our feet touch the high places. We are now riding on the high places of the earth. We are exercising the greatest kind of dominion over all the strongholds of the enemy. Whereas walking on the high places may be looked at as living in the fifth dimension, riding on them would refer to living in the sixth dimension.

This puts us in a whole new realm. It places us in a brand new dimension. We are now subscribing to a much higher law. We have a much greater power. We can override the lower dimensions where the work of the devil is carried out. We have dominion over the fourth dimension where spiritual warfare takes place.

Do It!

David said,

"Trust in the LORD [IN OTHER WORDS, MAKE HIM YOUR STRENGTH], and do good; so shalt thou dwell in the land, and verily thou shalt be fed [WE WOULD BE FED WITH THE HERITAGE OF JACOB].

"Delight thyself also in the LORD [ISAIAH TOLD US HOW TO DO THIS IN ISAIAH 58:13-14]; **and he shall give thee the desires of thine heart** [THE DESIRES OF OUR HEART WOULD BE INCLUDED IN THE BLESSINGS CONNECTED WITH RIDING THE HIGH PLACES OF THE EARTH].

"Commit thy way unto the LORD; trust also in him [KEEP YOUR CONFIDENCE IN HIM]; and he shall bring it to pass.

"Rest in the LORD, and wait patiently for him [THE HOLY GHOST IS STILL OUR REST; GOD IS STILL OUR REFUGE AND STRENGTH]: ... For yet a little while, and the wicked shall not be [THE WICKED ARE NOT INVINCIBLE; STRIP HIM DOWN AND SEE HIM FOR WHO HE IS]: ... But the meek shall inherit the earth; and shall delight themselves in the abundance of peace.

"... Their inheritance shall be forever [OUR VICTORY IS ETERNAL].

"... For such as be blessed of him shall inherit the earth;

"... Wait on the LORD, and keep his way, and he shall exalt thee to inherit the land" (Psalm 37:3-5, 7a, 10a, 11, 18b, 22a, 34a).

These are some of the promises we have if we exercise authority over the high places. And God does promise us that we can ride on the high places of the earth.

So let's make the Lord our strength. Let's go up to the high places. Let's go up to the high places to tear the devil's kingdom down. Let us fight with a killer's instinct. Let us strip Satan down and see him for who he is. Let us see our enemy without his "aura of invincibility." Let us fight and gain such a permanent victory that the enemy will be entirely consumed and not be able to recover.

Then let us possess the high places of the earth by exercising complete dominion over them. Let us ride with God on the high places of the earth. Let us inherit the promised land. Let us inherit the kingdom of God. Go ahead and reap the blessings of our inheritance. And let the inheritance be forever.

Books by David Sanzo
Order Form

	Qty.	Total

☐ Power to Tread on Serpents ($ 8.00) _____   _____
    Understanding and Using
    Spiritual Authority

☐ The Key to the Kingdom ($10.00)   _____   _____
    Beginning Your Reign
    in the Spirit

☐ The High Places ($10.00)   _____   _____
    Prayerfully Rising through the
    Seven Dimensions of Life

Please add 15% for shipping and handling.   _____

Total   _____

Name_____Address_____

City_____State_____Zip_____

Please send to:

Spirit of Life Ministries
4830 Morwanda Drive
Roanoke, VA 24017